Jane Austen's
Northanger Abbey

Adapted for the stage by
Matthew Francis

Samuel French — London
New York - Toronto - Hollywood

© 1997 BY MATTHEW FRANCIS

Rights of Performance by Amateurs are controlled by Samuel French Ltd, 52 Fitzroy Street, London W1P 6JR, and they, or their authorized agents, issue licences to amateurs on payment of a fee. **It is an infringement of the Copyright to give any performance or public reading of the play before the fee has been paid and the licence issued.**

The Royalty Fee indicated below is subject to contract and subject to variation at the sole discretion of Samuel French Ltd.

       Basic fee for each and every
          performance by amateurs   Code M
          in the British Isles

The Professional Repertory Rights in this play are controlled by SAMUEL FRENCH LTD.

The publication of this play does not imply that it is necessarily available for performance by amateurs or professionals, either in the British Isles or Overseas. Amateurs and professionals considering a production are strongly advised in their own interests to apply to the appropriate agents for consent before starting rehearsals or booking a theatre or hall.

ISBN 0 573 01849 9

Please see page iv for further copyright information

NORTHANGER ABBEY

First presented at Greenwich Theatre on 4th July 1996 with the following cast:

Mr Morland	Richard Lumsden
Mrs Morland	Karen Lewis
Mr James Morland	Luke Healey
Miss Catherine Morland	Sarah-Jane Holm
Mrs Allen	Celia Bannerman
Mrs Thorpe	Karen Lewis
Mr John Thorpe	Richard Lumsden
Miss Isabella Thorpe	Rebecca Saire
General Tilney	Michael Cronin
Captain Frederick Tilney	Charles Middrun
Mr Henry Tilney	James Wallace
Miss Eleanor Tilney	Karen Lewis
Annette	Celia Bannerman

Other parts played by the company

Piano music played by Mia Soteriou

Directed by Matthew Francis
Designed by Lez Brotherston
Lighting designed by Howard Harrison
Music by Mia Soteriou
Choreographed by Andrew George
Sound designed by Ed Brimley
Assistant Director Philip Wilson

COPYRIGHT INFORMATION

(See also page ii)

This play is fully protected under the Copyright Laws of the British Commonwealth of Nations, the United States of America and all countries of the Berne and Universal Copyright Conventions.

All rights including Stage, Motion Picture, Radio, Television, Public Reading, and Translation into Foreign Languages, are strictly reserved.

No part of this publication may lawfully be reproduced in ANY form or by any means — photocopying, typescript, recording (including video-recording), manuscript, electronic, mechanical, or otherwise — or be transmitted or stored in a retrieval system, without prior permission.

Licences for amateur performances are issued subject to the understanding that it shall be made clear in all advertising matter that the audience will witness an amateur performance; that the names of the authors of the plays shall be included on all programmes; and that the integrity of the authors' work will be preserved.

The Royalty Fee is subject to contract and subject to variation at the sole discretion of Samuel French Ltd.

In Theatres or Halls seating Four Hundred or more the fee will be subject to negotiation.

In Territories Overseas the fee quoted above may not apply. A fee will be quoted on application to our local authorized agent, or if there is no such agent, on application to Samuel French Ltd, London.

VIDEO-RECORDING OF AMATEUR PRODUCTIONS

Please note that the copyright laws governing video-recording are extremely complex and that it should not be assumed that any play may be video-recorded for whatever purpose without first obtaining the permission of the appropriate agents. The fact that a play is published by Samuel French Ltd does not indicate that video rights are available or that Samuel French Ltd controls such rights.

CHARACTERS

Mr Morland
Mrs Morland
Mr James Morland
Miss Catherine Morland
Mrs Allen
Mrs Thorpe
Mr John Thorpe
Miss Isabella Thorpe
General Tilney
Captain Frederick Tilney
Mr Henry Tilney
Miss Eleanor Tilney
Annette
Montoni
Count de Vereza
Dimity O' Flynne

Servants
Gothic characters

The action of the play takes place in various settings in Bath and Gloucestershire, and in the imaginary world of Udolpho

Period — Regency

PRODUCTION NOTES

TWO LEVELS OF REALITY

Northanger Abbey is about the dangers of fiction. Catherine Morland — brought up in a sleepy provincial parsonage — is suddenly introduced to the complicated world of a "season" at Bath, and tries to make sense of it by constant reference to the gothic romances which have been her all-consuming passion at home. Believing "society" to be very much as Mrs Anne Radcliffe describes it, she makes a number of alarming miscalculations about personalities and relationships, but survives — thanks principally to the indulgence of her author.

In our production at Greenwich, we established the shadowy world of Mrs Radcliffe's *The Mysteries of Udolpho* from the start of the play, and at crucial moments, with Catherine under pressure and fresh circumstances demanding that she take a "view", we allowed her to see Henry Tilney, or John Thorpe or the housekeeper at Northanger Abbey as characters from the spooky world of Udolpho.

We staged the play on a brilliant set by Lez Brotherston, with walls of elegant, gauzy white curtaining that in daylight opened on to picturesque landscapes, but at night could twist and float and suddenly reveal the shadowy renaissance world of masks and daggers and ominous threats to a maiden's peace of mind. Udolpho "takes over" at a number of points in the play: sometimes for a few moments, sometimes for longer stretches — especially when Catherine actually arrives in Northanger. These gothic interludes can best be accomplished simply, by a dimming of the light, a whisper of music, eerie sound effects, the addition of a high-collared cloak to a costume, the use of a mask, the flicker of a candle. It's very important that the gothic world can dissolve in a moment: Catherine blinks, and it's all gone. Cumbersome devices won't do at all.

STAGING THE PLAY

The play takes place in a large number of locations: at Fullerton, at Pulteney Street, at the Upper Rooms, at the Theatre Royal, in the street, on a drive, all over Northanger Abbey, and of course, in various dim and dusty rooms at Udolpho.

This adaptation cannot work if any attempt is undertaken to substantially recreate all these locations. Simplicity is the key. Our white curtains could close completely for a claustrophobic interior, or gather in a number of different configurations to suggest the ruched grandeur of a ballroom or theatre, or open on to sublime landscapes — painted on the walls of the theatre itself. John Thorpe's carriage consisted of two chairs and a travelling rug and Henry Tilney clip-clopping two coconut halves. Tilney's own carriage at the start of Act II had a recorded sound effect, and Tilney carried a riding crop. The melt from Udolpho into Fullerton at the very start of the play was simple and immensely effective: the Morland family — who had been providing some of the ghostly sound effects for Catherine's gothic journey through Udolpho — were sitting behind the great dark gauze which she so fearfully tugged down. Lights switched from ghostly night-time to summer afternoon, creaks and groans and Mia Soteriou's wonderfully potent music gave way to birds chirruping and the sound of children playing, the gauze was pulled down through a tiny hole in the stage, and — voilà! — an instant transformation.

DOUBLING

We presented the play with eight actors. Ten or twelve would have made the busy social landscapes at Bath a shade more convincing, but there is always pleasure for an audience in seeing a small group of performers manage every part. Mrs Morland was very busy — turning into Mrs Thorpe and then into Eleanor Tilney. Mr Morland became John Thorpe; General Tilney made a brief appearance as Dimity O'Flynne the dressmaker (as well — of course — as the terrifying Montoni). Everyone took part in the dancing, if they weren't actually engaged in a scene downstage. Everyone took a turn at narrating: sometimes in character, sometimes as "observer".

There are only eleven principal characters in *Northanger Abbey*. Directors might chose to import children for the Fullerton scenes, people Udolpho with a larger number of rude mercenaries and unscrupulous hitmen, fill the Upper Rooms with a greater crush of dancers. But it's not essential.

Montoni MUST be played by the General, and the Count de Vereza by Henry Tilney. It worked very well for Mrs Allen to play Annette.

With only eight actors, the company are more or less on stage all the time. It is not envisaged however, that the company MUST be on stage all the time. Indeed, it would be confusing — in a show where not all the actors are playing three or four parts — for Henry or Catherine or Isabella suddenly to turn up as background interest. With a larger cast it certainly wouldn't be necessary.

DANCING

Dances are a very important part of Northanger Abbey. Andrew George was our choreographer. His work was based in formal tradition, but he elaborated or decorated the original patterns to suit particular scenes and allow dialogue between partners.

For the young girls in *Northanger Abbey*, dancing is the ultimate diversion: allowing them to display their skill, flirt, have some physical contact with the opposite sex, show off their beautiful gowns, be the centre of attention, recruit husbands. It is not a casual pastime, though it is an exuberant one. It commands the same focus that you might expect today from an Olympic gymnast.

Matthew Francis

MUSIC PLOT FOR NORTHANGER ABBEY

The music for NORTHANGER ABBEY was derived from two sources. The first was a specially written score by Mia Soteriou, the second was a selection of eighteenth century dances — mostly by Joseph Haydn.

Mia composed all the "atmosphere", underscore and mood music in the play — as well as the music for the "ballet" in Act II. Mia's music was composed for piano, and is available on DAT and on cassette. Enquiries for use of this music should be made to Rachel Daniels at LONDON MANAGEMENT, 2-4 Noel Street, London W1V 3RB (0171 287 9000).

Apart from the ballet, there are thirteen dances written into the script, only one of them longer than a minute. It seemed inappropriate to use solo piano for these, and hardly less so to introduce large-scale orchestral music into the simple elegance of Jane Austen's world. In any case, orchestral work sounded unduly grand in a comparatively small-scale adaptation.

Our final choice for these dances was — mostly — music by Haydn composed for a small band of a dozen or so players. It had the right intimacy and merriment; it seemed to be the right scale for our purposes. The pieces we used are as follows:

Page 10:	2nd of five Contredanses. (Hob IX: 29). Joseph Haydn
Page 15	1st of six Minuetti da Ballo. (Hob IX: 4). Joseph Haydn
Page 16:	Quadrille (Hob IX: 24). Joseph Haydn
Page 22:	1st of five Contredanses. (Hob IX: 29). Joseph Haydn
Page 24:	1st of six Allemandes (Hob IX: 12). Joseph Haydn
Page 28:	4th of five Contredanses (Hob IX: 4) Joseph Haydn
Page 30:	*Bobbing Joan.* Arranged and played by The City Waites.
Page 41:	Music by Mia Soteriou

Page 42:	2nd of six Allemandes (Hob IX: 12). Joseph Haydn
Page 45:	Music by Mia Soteriou
Page 46:	Music by Mia Soteriou
Page 47:	Quadrille (Hob IX: 24). Joseph Haydn
Page 67:	Music by Mia Soteriou
Page 79:	4th of five Contredanses (Hob IX: 4). Joseph Haydn

The music by Haydn is all available on the CD *Haydn: Zingarese / Landler / Nocturnes* recorded by the Ensemble Bella Musica de Vienne on Harmonia Mundi: HMA 1901057.

Bobbing Joan is available on the CD *The Merry Milkmaid* recorded by The City Waites, on Past Times: SAMHC 009.

Matthew Francis

N.B. Please refer to the Effects Plot p.85 as this includes music cues.

A licence issued by Samuel French Ltd to perform this play does not include permission to use the Incidental music specified in this copy. Where the place of performance is already licensed by the PERFORMING RIGHT SOCIETY a return of the music used must be made to them. If the place of performance is not so licensed then application should be made to the Performing Right Society, 29 Berners Street, London W1.

A separate and additional licence from PHONOGRAPHIC PERFORMANCES LTD, Ganton House, Ganton Street, London W1 is needed whenever commercial recordings are used.

ACT I

Prologue

Udolpho

Music. A sudden rush of candlelight

Catherine arrives, clutching a pile of novels. Isabella is beside her, holding a three-candle candelabra. Flames flicker and dance: shadows loom and shift

The two girls are nervous, excited. They fling themselves down

Isabella Have you gone on with *Udolpho*?
Catherine Yes, I have been reading it ever since I woke; and I am got to the black veil!
Isabella Are you indeed? How awful! How delightful! Oh, I would not tell you what is behind the black veil for the world! Are you not wild to know?
Catherine Oh yes, quite. What can it be? But do not tell me, I would not be told upon any account. I know it must be a skeleton. I am sure it is Laurentina's skeleton. Oh, I am delighted with the book! I should like to spend my whole life in reading it!
Isabella When you have finished *Udolpho*, we will read *The Italian* together; and I have made out a list of ten or twelve more of the same kind for you.
Catherine Have you indeed! How glad I am! What are they all?
Isabella I will read you their names directly: here they are in my pocket book.

Her list is accompanied by appropriately Gothic sound effects, perhaps managed on stage by the company: howls, whispering voices, laughs, chiming bells ...

Castle of Wolfenbach, Clermont, Mysterious Warnings, Necromancer of the Black Forest, Midnight Bell ...
Catherine Ah! I have read *Midnight Bell* ...
Isabella (*from memory*) "It rings for thee, Sir Bertram, it rings for thee and for all thy race!"

Catherine squeals

Orphan of the Rhine, A Sicilian Romance, The Castle of Otranto and...

Catherine (*breathless*) Yes ...?
Isabella (*with maximum effect*) Horrid Mysteries!
Catherine Those will last us some time.
Isabella Yes. It is so odd to me that you should never have read *Udolpho* before ...
Catherine I will not hear a thing beyond the first volume. Do not tell me one thing that happens at Udolpho. I would not know about the dreadful black veil!
Isabella (*mischievous; half reading, half from memory*) "Emily stood at the door in an attitude of hesitation, with the light held up to show the chamber, but the feeble rays spread through not half of it." (*She blows out the first of the three candles in the candelabra*)

Shadows dance. A twinkle of spooky notes

(*Increasing the tension*) "What furniture there was appeared to be almost as old as the rooms, and retained an appearance of grandeur, though covered with dust, and dropping to pieces with the damps and with age." (*She blows out the second candle*)

Now it is very spooky

"The walls of the chamber were hung with pictures, and though the candle guttered and its flame almost died, she passed the light hastily over several of these, until — until she came to one concealed by a veil of black silk!" (*She blows out the last candle*)

The Light goes out on Isabella and she disappears

Another woman appears; this is Annette, Emily's servant in Udolpho, *dressed in a suggestion of seventeenth-century costume. She speaks with a dramatic French accent*

Annette (*screaming*) Holy Virgin! What can this mean? This is surely the picture they told me of at Venice!
Catherine And what have you heard of this picture to terrify you so, Annette?
Annette Nothing ma'm'selle, I have heard nothing; only let us find the way out. If Signor Montoni should chance upon us here!

Other voices call Montoni's name, which echoes through unseen halls and chambers

Catherine What have you heard that makes you so eager to go?

Act I, Prologue

Annette I have heard there is something very dreadful belonging to it!
Catherine (*awed, terrified*) What? What?
Annette That it has been covered up in black, covered ever since — ever since ——
Catherine Ever since WHAT?
Annette (*backing away into the shadows*) And that nobody has dared to look at it for many years — and that it somehow has to do with Signora Laurentina ——

We hear a plaintive cry from a far-off dungeon: "Signora Laurentina"

— she who owned this castle before Signor Montoni ——

And again his name is echoed

— came to the possession of it. I cannot ... I dare not ... I will not spend another moment ...

Annette vanishes, her voice echoing down distant corridors

Catherine I cannot stay a night within this room. Signor Montoni will understand. He will not expose one under his protection to the doubts and terrors of a chamber such as this. Surely within his fierce and haughty breast ——

Suddenly, Montoni is there: a sinister, dark, scheming figure, like the portrait of a seventeenth-century Venetian politician

Catherine turns, sees Montoni and screams

Montoni (*horribly*) I have no time to attend to these idle whims. That chamber was prepared for you, and you must rest contented with it!
Catherine Dear Sir ——
Montoni If you will not release yourself from the slavery of these fears, at least forbear to torment others by the mention of them. Endeavour to strengthen your mind. No existence is more contemptible than that which is embittered by *fear*.
Catherine By what right do you address me thus? By what right have you brought me to this place?
Montoni By what right? By the right of my will! I now remind you for the last time, that you are a stranger in a foreign country, and that it is in your interest to make me your friend; you know the means; if you compel me to be your enemy, I will venture to tell you that the punishment will exceed your expectations. You may know that I am not to be trifled with!

And the Light goes out on him. A door bangs. Distant echoes, groans and the anguished cries of "Signora Laurentina" are heard throughout the next speech. Music ratchets up the tension

Catherine (*delighted/terrified*) She walked through rooms, obscure and desolate, where no footsteps had passed, probably for many years, and remembered the strange history of Signora Laurentina. Horror occupied her mind, but she resolved to examine the veiled painting. She entered her chamber and went towards the picture, which appeared to be enclosed in a frame of uncommon size, that hung in a dark part of the room. Terror seized her. She paused again, and then, with a trembling hand, *pulled at the veil!* (*She reaches up and pulls at a cloth that flutters down on top of her. See Production Note: "Staging the Play"*)

The Lights snap to Fullerton, the village and the house where Catherine and her family live. Birds twitter, children squeal and giggle in other rooms, a dog barks

Mrs Morland shoos Catherine and bustles about. Mrs Allen follows her. Mr Morland searches for his paper

Scene 1

Fullerton

Mrs Morland (*scolding*) My best muslin! Have a care! Catherine Morland — what a shatter-brained creature you are to be sure! How you dash at a thing!
Catherine Oh Mother, I am sorry. Very, very sorry...
Mr Morland (*to the audience*) No one who had ever seen Catherine Morland in her infancy would have supposed her born to be a heroine.
Catherine Please, I beg you, Mother, do not be cross — tell me your secret! Mrs Allen, do not let her keep me in suspense.
Mrs Morland (*ignoring Catherine*) We had thought you quite grown up at last; almost a lady, had we not, Mr Morland?
Catherine Mother!
Mr Morland (*to the audience*) Her father was a clergyman, and a very respectable man ... and he was not in the least addicted to locking up his daughters.
Mrs Allen Indeed, Mrs Morland, she is grown into the sweetest thing that ever lived. Her cheeks are plump, her colour good, and her complexion — almost improved ...
Mrs Morland Perhaps we cannot, after all, tell you of Mrs Allen's kind invitation.

Act I, Scene 1

Catherine Invitation? To whom? To *me,* or merely to the family?
Mrs Morland Are we no longer fit to be invited with you, Catherine? Indeed, I shall most certainly not tell you now!
Catherine You *must,* you must tell me! I am seventeen and have a right to know. Oh, I shall die if you do not tell me *now*!
Mrs Morland You were ever and always a young dizzy-head, your face in the mud, your skirts in a tangle.
Mrs Allen But she has listened to my advice about dress, and looked... well enough at Mrs Kingsley's tea ...
Mrs Morland *(to Mrs Allen)* Her three brothers lacked a sister to teach them manners and good behaviour, but lo! my Catherine turns out to be the greatest savage of the tribe, fit only for a bat and a ball and a game of cricket. Is it not so, Mr Morland?
Mr Morland *(carefully)* To be sure, she cannot draw, and can hardly play "Bo Peep" upon the piano ⸺
Catherine Father! I practise every day!
Mr Morland Her French is distressing, her proficiency at arithmetic unremarkable ⸺
Catherine *(tragically)* Oh Mrs Allen, how I am wronged!
Mr Morland But ⸺ *(a beat)* ⸺ our Catherine grows quite a good-looking girl. She is almost pretty today.
Catherine *(amazed)* Is it true?
Mr Morland And she *reads* a very great deal...
Mrs Allen Much useful knowledge is to be gained from reading. What is it that you read Catherine?
Mrs Morland *(laconically)* Novels!
Mrs Allen Novels?
Mr Morland *Novels.*
Mrs Morland *(promptly)* I *seldom* look into novels...
Mr Morland Do not imagine that *I* read novels!
Mrs Allen *(after a moment)* What novels do you read, Catherine?
Catherine Horrid ones.
Mr Morland In which Cecilia or Julia or Emily walk out in the woods to an ancient pavilion overlooking the bay of Naples, where they meet a young lord whose origin is mysteriously unknown ...
Mrs Allen Such adventures are rare indeed in Fullerton.
Catherine They are *impossible*! There is no young man in all the country with a secret worth discovering. Really, Wiltshire is the dullest place.
Mrs Allen Duller than Bath?
Catherine *(in a whisper)* Than Bath?
Mrs Allen *(confidentially)* If adventures will not befall a young lady in her own village, then she might seek them in Bath ...
Mrs Morland My little scatter-head would never manage in a great town like *Bath*. She would not know which way to turn or where to go or how

to dress. I think that she will never find her way beyond the bottom of our garden. What do you say, Mr Morland?

Mr Morland I say: torment the girl no longer. Come, Mrs Allen, tell Catherine your plan.

Mrs Allen In brief. Mr Allen has been ordered to Bath for the benefit of his gouty constitution. We are fond of you, Catherine, and have asked your parents if you may go with us.

Catherine (*thunderstruck*) To Bath?

Mrs Allen For six weeks residence.

Catherine Six weeks! Oh, Mother, Father — may I go?

Mrs Morland Well...

Mr Morland Well...

A beat

Mr Morland ⎫
Mrs Morland ⎭ (*together*) Of course! OF COURSE!

Catherine (*thrilled*) BATH!

Music, activity, preparations

Mrs Allen (*to the audience*) The journey was performed with suitable quietness, and uneventful safety.

Catherine (*to the audience*) Within two days, they arrived!

SCENE 2

Mrs Allen Gets Ready

Bath

Distant music and bustle

Mrs Allen We shall not venture into society at once. We shall spend our first three or four days learning what is mostly worn ——

And in sweep Dimity O'Flynne, the dressmaker, and his assistant. Through the next scene, they help Catherine and Mrs Allen get out of their coats and into newly tailored finery

—— then we shall pull our old gowns to pieces and make them up again for the latest fashion.

Catherine (*alarmed*) Three or four days?

Act I, Scene 3

Dimity (*to the audience*) And they were soon settled in comfortable lodgings in Pulteney Street.
Mrs Allen I have brought five gowns that may be worked on, and shall purchase five *more* in the morning!
Catherine And *then* shall we visit the Upper Rooms?
Dimity (*to the audience*) Mrs Allen had the air of a gentlewoman, a great deal of quiet, inactive good temper, and a trifling turn of mind. Dress was her passion.
Mrs Allen (*choosing fabric*) Oh *yes*! (*To Catherine*) Half boots become a young ankle well. I shall buy you half boots as a present. Nankin galoshed with black looks *very* well...
Catherine Dear, dear Mrs Allen! And shall I wear them to the Upper Rooms?
Mrs Allen (*breathless with enthusiasm*) See, child! A round dress of worked muslin with satin trimming: the newest fashion! I saw a French lady with two servants wear it yesterday! Two falls of lace on the skirt, a Gloucester turban, white gauze laid on very full, ostrich feathers — you see? — falling to the left ...
Catherine (*enraptured*) It is beautiful, beautiful!
Mrs Allen Then you will need a tunic, and a new cap from Jebbs — gold net I fancy ——
Catherine And shall we visit the Upper Rooms *tonight, dear* Mrs Allen?
Dimity (*to the audience*) Mrs Allen was so long in dressing, that they did not enter the ballroom till late. And so it was that night, and upon the Wednesday, and again upon the Friday!

Scene 3

The Upper Rooms

The music and noise of the Upper Rooms burst in on them

People enter, buffeting Catherine and Mrs Allen. They cling to one another

Catherine (*gasping*) So many people!
1st Gent (*to his friend*) Rather quiet this evening...
Mrs Allen My lace will tear!
2nd Gent Always the same faces.
Catherine I can see *nothing*...
1st Lady Tom Musgrave dances with Miss Carr!
Mrs Allen Follow closely...
2nd Lady Who is the particular friend of *my* very particular friend.
Catherine Just as before! There are no seats!

1st Gent The best people have the front benches ...
Mrs Allen Perhaps at the top ...
1st Lady The Osbornes and the Blakes and the Watsons ...
Catherine They are full. Just as before!
2nd Lady And the Nortons and the Heywoods and the Hunters of *course*!
Mrs Allen Such a crowd!
Catherine Such a sight!
Mrs Allen Such a change from Fullerton!
Catherine Introduce me!
Mrs Allen If only...
1st Gent Not a pretty girl to be seen ...
Catherine (*indignant*) Yet Catherine was in very good looks ——
2nd Gent The pretty girls are all with their partners ...
Catherine — and had the company only seen her three years before ——
1st Gent Or gone away.
Catherine — they would now have thought her exceedingly handsome!
1st Lady I feel sorry for her.
Mrs Allen I wish you could dance.
2nd Lady She is quite alone.
Mrs Allen Young people should dance.
1st Lady I have danced all evening.
Mrs Allen I wish you could get a partner ——
2nd Lady *I* have had quite enough of it...
Mrs Allen — but we know no-one.
Catherine (*cheerfully*) It does not matter.
Mrs Allen The tea room!
Catherine Oh.
Mrs Allen Come with me!
Catherine Yes.
Mrs Allen This way!
Catherine Catherine began to feel ——
Mrs Allen We can sit down!
Catherine — something of disappointment ...

SCENE 4

Nothing Happens

They sit. The music quietens. They stare out at the audience

Mrs Allen (*inspecting her ensemble*) My gown is safe! What a relief. It would have been very shocking to have it torn, would it not? It is such a delicate muslin. For my part, I have not seen anything I like so well in the whole room, I assure you.

Act I, Scene 5

Catherine (*excited, frustrated*) How uncomfortable it is not to know a single person.
Mrs Allen Yes, my dear, it is very uncomfortable indeed. I wish we had a large acquaintance here.
Catherine I wish we had *any* ... It would be somebody to go to.
Mrs Allen If we knew *anybody* we would join them directly. The Skinners were here last year. I wish they were here now.
Catherine But dear Mrs Allen, are you sure there is nobody you know in all this multitude of people?
Mrs Allen I don't upon my word. I wish I did. I wish I had a large acquaintance here with all my heart. Then I should get you a partner.
Catherine I think you must know *somebody*...
Mrs Allen (*not hearing her*) But have you had an agreeable ball, my dear?
Catherine Very agreeable indeed!
Mrs Allen I wish you could have danced. How glad I should have been to have seen the Skinners, or if the Parrys had come. You might have danced with George Parry. You would have had a partner. But heaven be praised, my gown is safe!

SCENE 5

Catherine's Reverie

Mrs Allen prattles on

A figure in Venetian mask and sixteenth century cloak approaches from the shadows of Catherine's imagination. (In the next scene this figure turns out to be Tilney.) The Lights flicker and dip. A mysterious tremor of music ...

Venetian/Tilney The Count de Vereza advanced towards her across the room. His person was graceful, yet manly; his mind accomplished, and manners elegant ...
Catherine Her heart dilated with pleasure and diffused over her features an expression of pure and complacent delight ...
Venetian/Tilney That heart must be either fickle or insensible which can boast of freedom in the presence of the Lady Julia ...
Catherine He led her forth. The grace of her step, and the elegant symmetry of her figure raised in the assembly a gentle murmur of applause ...

SCENE 6

A Dance With Mr Tilney

And we hear the applause. A second man appears and removes the mysterious figure's mask and cloak, revealing Tilney. Catherine surfaces from her daydream

The Upper Rooms again. Mrs Allen is staring at her young companion

Mrs Allen (*concerned*) Catherine! Catherine! Are you feeling faint? Here is Mr King, master of the Upper Rooms, come to introduce a young man. His name is Mr Tilney.
Catherine Oh — forgive me ...
Mrs Allen (*sotto voce*) A clergyman. Of very respectable family. From Gloucestershire.
Tilney You were in a dream, Miss Morland. Now that you have awakened, I trust I do not seem too disagreeable a reality.
Catherine (*amused but confused*) No, not too disagreeable. I mean, not at all disagreeable ...
Tilney I believe that the pleasantest sensation in the Upper Rooms, Miss Morland, is remembering that soon enough one will leave them. Shall we attempt to dance? It may take us nearer to the door.

A dance. Other ladies and gentlemen join Catherine and Tilney for the first set piece of the play. [See Music Plot]

At last Catherine and Tilney return to sit down. Music plays in the background

Scene 7

The First Conversation

Tilney I have been hitherto very remiss, madam, in the proper attentions of a partner here. I have not yet asked you how long you have been in Bath, whether you were ever here before, and how you like the place altogether. I have been very negligent. But are you now at leisure to satisfy me in these particulars?
Catherine You need not give yourself that trouble, sir.
Tilney No trouble I assure you, madam. (*He affects ingratiation*) Have you been long in Bath, madam?
Catherine (*almost giggling*) About a week sir.
Tilney (*amazed*) Really?
Catherine Why should you be surprised, sir?
Tilney (*his own voice*) Why indeed! But some emotion must appear to be raised by your reply, and surprise is more easily assumed than any other. Now — let us go on. (*Ingratiatingly*) Were you never here before, madam?
Catherine Never, sir.
Tilney Indeed! Have you been to the theatre?
Catherine Yes, sir. I was at the play on Tuesday.

Act I, Scene 7   11

Tilney To the concert?
Catherine Yes, sir, on Thursday.
Tilney And are you altogether pleased with Bath?
Catherine Yes, I like it very well.
Tilney Now, I must give one smirk, and then we may be rational again... (*He smirks*)

Catherine laughs

(*Apparently grave*) I see what you think of me. I shall make but a poor figure in your journal tomorrow.
Catherine My journal?
Tilney Yes, I know exactly what you will say: "Friday, went to the Upper Rooms; wore my sprigged muslin robe with blue trimmings, plain black shoes, appeared to much advantage; but was strangely harassed by a queer, half-witted man, who would make me dance with him, and distressed me by his nonsense."
Catherine Indeed, I shall say no such thing.
Tilney Shall I tell you what you ought to say?
Catherine If you please.
Tilney "I danced with a very agreeable young man. Had a great deal of conversation with him; seems a most extraordinary genius — hope I may know more of him ..."
Catherine But perhaps I keep no journal.
Tilney Perhaps you are not sitting in this room and I am not sitting by you! Not keep a journal! How are your absent cousins to understand the tenor of your life in Bath without one? How are your various dresses to be remembered, and the particular curl of your hair to be described, without having recourse to a journal? It is this delightful habit of journalizing which largely contributes to the easy style of writing for which ladies are so generally celebrated. Everybody allows that the talent of writing agreeable letters is peculiarly female.
Catherine I have sometimes thought whether ladies do write so much better letters than gentlemen! That is, I should not think the superiority was always on our side.
Tilney As far as I have had opportunity of judging, it appears to me that the usual style of letter-writing among women is faultless, except in three particulars.
Catherine And what are they?
Tilney A general deficiency of subject, a total inattention to stops, and a very frequent ignorance of grammar.
Catherine Upon my word! You do not think too highly of us in that way!
Tilney It is no more true that women write better letters than men, than that they play better duets, or draw better landscapes. In every power of which

taste is the foundation, excellence is pretty fairly divided between the sexes.

Scene 8

Tilney On Muslin

Mrs Allen arrives in a flap

Mrs Allen My dear Catherine, do take this pin out of my sleeve; I am afraid it has torn a hole already. I shall be quite sorry if it has, for this is a favourite gown, though it cost but nine shillings a yard ...

Catherine complies

Tilney That is exactly what I would have guessed it, madam.
Mrs Allen Do you understand muslins, sir?
Tilney Particularly well; my sister has often trusted me in the choice of a gown. I bought one for her the other day, and it was pronounced to be a prodigious bargain by every lady who saw it. I gave but five shillings a yard for it, and a true Indian muslin.
Mrs Allen (*amazed and delighted*) Men commonly take so little notice of these things. And pray, sir, what do you think of Miss Morland's gown?
Tilney It is very pretty, madam, but I do not think it will wash well: I am afraid it will fray.
Catherine How can you be so ... (*she nearly says "strange"*)
Mrs Allen I am quite of your opinion, sir, and so I told Miss Morland when she bought it.
Catherine Mrs Allen...
Tilney But then you know, madam, muslin always turns to some account or other; Miss Morland will get enough out of it for a cloak, or a cap, or a handkerchief. Muslin can never be said to be wasted ...

Scene 9

Mrs Thorpe

From another part of the stage comes a voice, a loud, friendly, woman's voice, that of Mrs Thorpe

Mrs Thorpe (*off*) Excuse me! Excuse me! Madam!
Mrs Allen (*to Tilney*) Is she addressing me?
Catherine Do you know her, Mrs Allen?

Act I, Scene 9   13

Mrs Allen I have no acquaintance in Bath. Would that I did.
Mrs Thorpe (*off*)   I cannot be mistaken; is not your name Allen?
Mrs Allen (*helplessly*) What am I to do?
Tilney If your name *is* Allen, then declare yourself.
Mrs Allen (*summoning courage*) I *am* Mrs Allen!
Mrs Thorpe (*off*)   Formerly Vernon?
Mrs Allen (*in astonishment*) Indeed!

Mrs Thorpe advances

Mrs Thorpe It is a long time since I had the pleasure of seeing you. My name is Thorpe!
Mrs Allen (*momentarily bewildered*) Thorpe? Thorpe?
Mrs Thorpe Formerly Tomlinson!
Mrs Allen Formerly Tomlinson... (*She is suddenly animated*) But of course! My dear Mrs Thorpe, this is a happy day. How have you been these ten years?
Mrs Thorpe Twenty!
Mrs Allen *Fifteen.*
Mrs Thorpe Indeed. You look the very same!
Mrs Allen And so do you. *Hardly* altered. The light here is so very poor ...

And Mrs Thorpe and Mrs Allen move away; their chatter is only occasionally audible

Tilney (*to Catherine*) What are you thinking of so earnestly?
Catherine I was not thinking of anything.
Tilney That is artful and deep to be sure; but I had rather be told at once that you will not tell me.
Mrs Thorpe How time has slipped away since we were last together!
Mrs Allen I have often taken up the pen to write...
Catherine (*answering Tilney*) Well then   — I will not.
Tilney Thank you. For now we shall soon be acquainted, as I am authorized to tease you on this subject whenever we meet.
Mrs Allen Catherine!

Tilney slips away during the following; Mrs Thorpe and Mrs Allen approach Catherine

Tilney (*in a whisper*) And nothing in the world advances intimacy so much...
Mrs Allen Catherine, this is my very old dear friend, Mrs Thorpe.
Mrs Thorpe Formerly Tomlinson.
Mrs Allen Mrs Thorpe, this is Miss Morland, the daughter of a good friend at Fullerton.

Mrs Thorpe Fullerton. Yes. And how is Mr Allen?
Mrs Allen (*this is going to be a long answer*) Ah, well ——
Mrs Thorpe (*determined that it won't be*) Mr Thorpe, as you know ...
Mrs Allen Alas.
Mrs Thorpe Alas; but my children are a consolation and a joy. Your own?
Mrs Allen Alas.
Mrs Thorpe (*impervious to the reply*) *Edward* is still at Merchant Taylor's — wants to be a surgeon, warm and easy, clever with the knife — *William* at sea — brave and redoubtable, a valiant foe to England's enemies, skilled with a sword; and *John* ——
Catherine — is at Oxford!
Mrs Thorpe Yes — why, yes. But how ... ?
Catherine He is my brother's close companion. John Thorpe.
Mrs Thorpe (*delightedly*) Of course: Morland, James Morland. And now I come to look at you ——
Mrs Allen Another happy chance! Is your son with you, Mrs Thorpe?
Mrs Thorpe Arriving any day from Oxford. You shall meet him, Catherine. Clever, impetuous, direct ——
Mrs Allen (*suddenly rivetted*) I vow the lace on your pelisse is very like that upon my own — dear Mrs Thorpe. A little less intricate, perhaps. I had this lace from William Healy's. Mr Allen calls it extravagance, but I think details on a gown are so important ——
Mrs Thorpe (*cutting across her*) Here comes my eldest girl. My dear Mrs Allen, is she not a fine young woman?

SCENE 10

Isabella

And indeed she is. Stylish, graceful, fashionable. A little older than Catherine. This is Isabella, who approaches

Isabella Mother.
Mrs Thorpe My dear, today has seen the happiest reunion. You know that I have spoken of a much-loved school-fellow and confidante, the intimate companion of my childhood days. Behold! Mrs Allen! And this, Mrs Allen, is my daughter Isabella, the handsomest of all my children!
Isabella What a very great pleasure, Mrs Allen.
Mrs Thorpe And here, another pleasing circumstance. Mrs Allen's young companion is none other than Miss Catherine Morland, and Miss Morland is ——
Isabella (*pleased and amused*) — James Morland's sister! How excessively like her brother Miss Morland is!

Act I, Scene 11   15

Mrs Thorpe The very picture of him indeed!
Isabella I should have known you anywhere for his sister. I consider you at once my friend on his account!
Catherine Dear Miss Thorpe!
Isabella Dear, dear Miss Morland!

SCENE 11

Isabella and Catherine

Music starts (See Music Plot)

Isabella The first minuet!

During the following, Isabella dances round Catherine, then the two of them dance together. The second set piece

> Would it not be wonderful if you and I became the closest friends? (*Confidentially*) I will not share you with another soul. Your brother, Mr Morland, is the sweetest gentleman. My brother is devoted to him.

Catherine So is James to John!
Isabella And shall we make a resolution to outshine them in devotion? I feel instantly a warmth towards you quite unlike the feelings that are common between strangers.
Catherine And I for you!
Isabella You have not been to Bath before, I think — at least, I have not seen you here — and it is quite impossible that had we met I should not now remember it. Why, this is only the fourth year Mama has brought us here ——
Catherine (*amazed*) The fourth!
Isabella The fourth! And, truth to tell, I weary of the place. Tunbridge is more elegant, less crowded, closer to London. The rooms are not oppressive and the gentlemen much more attentive than in Bath. What do you think?
Catherine I have been in Bath a week, and danced but once ...
Isabella Once in a week? It is a scandal. You, quite the prettiest and sweetest creature in the town, dance only once! The men are *blind*. I think your petticoat the smartest thing; the trim is charming, and the cap, so delicate ... Is gold net still allowable? I think it is. And, if not, you alone may sway the town and bring the fashion back!
Catherine I know so little of fashion.
Isabella (*suddenly*) Look at those two ancient quizzes over there; one bonnet like an oyster basket, the other like a garden trug.
Catherine But the lady next to them is very smart, I think. The satin jacket is the nicest blue!

Isabella Too bright and cut too long. The sleeves should be short and full. (*She scans the room*) Ah! Only look there! No! Do not stare. You see the gentleman in black; cream-coloured breeches, longish nose ...
Catherine I see him. Why?
Isabella He has a secret with the woman over here in green. Do you not see the smiles that go between them?

Catherine looks at one, and then the other

Catherine No.
Isabella I have noticed her before. And in that dress. Mrs Sage Green, I call her. But I have not seen her simper at the man in black until today. What is his history, I wonder?
Catherine (*bravely*) Perhaps, like Montoni in *Udolpho*, he has a wife that wearies him, and she is kept away, back in some dreary house, deep in the country ——
Isabella You know *Udolpho*?
Catherine Only the first volume.
Isabella I have read it twice. The second time entirely at night! (*She takes Catherine's hands*) How fortunate that we have met. I know that we shall like each other always. This new acquaintance is the most delightful of my life. Come, tell me everything about yourself. Leave nothing out!
Catherine Dear Miss Thorpe.
Isabella *Isabella*. Catherine?
Catherine Of course!

SCENE 12

An Interval at the Theatre

Music. The third set piece. The two girls speak as they dance

Isabella (*to the audience*) The progress of the friendship between Catherine and Isabella was quick as its beginning had been warm, and they passed rapidly through every gradation of increasing tenderness.
Catherine (*to the audience*) But Mr Tilney was not at the concert that evening, nor at the Pump Room on the following day. He was nowhere to be seen.
Isabella Eight or nine days passed. Every search for him was unsuccessful — in morning lounges, or evening assemblies...
Catherine He was a subject in which she often indulged with her fair friend, at the concert, in the Pump Room, at the milliners, on their Sunday Promenade, and even, during an interval, at the theatre.

Act I, Scene 13

They arrive at theatre seats; a box at the Theatre Royal. US, *we see a glimpse of the stage. A buzz of spectators. Musical instruments tuning up*

Isabella Continue to think of him, dear Catherine. I know he likes you.
Catherine How?
Isabella I feel it. You have described a charming young man, and if he is as you describe him, how could he be other than delighted with my dear Catherine?
Catherine He did not mention that his stay in Bath would be so short. It is mysterious. What am I to think? Has he been called away? Did I offend him? Perhaps he is ill!
Isabella He is a clergyman? Ah well. Perhaps a sudden death called him away. An unexpected funeral. (*A beat*) I like him the better for being a clergyman. I must confess myself very partial to the profession. (*She sighs*)
Catherine My brother James will be a clergyman ...
Isabella (*another sigh*) Yes. (*She sits up suddenly*) Oh look! There! Miss Andrews, waving. (*She waves back*) A sweet girl, one of the sweetest creatures in the world. I wish you knew Miss Andrews, you would be delighted with her. I think her as beautiful as an angel, and I am so vexed with the men for not admiring her! I scold them all amazingly about it.
Catherine Scold them! Do you scold them for not admiring her?
Isabella Yes, that I do. There is nothing I would not do for those who are really my friends. I have no notion of loving people by halves, it is not in my nature. My attachments are always excessively strong. Now, if I were to hear anyone speak slightingly of you, I should fire up in a moment. But that is not at all likely, for you are just the kind of girl to be a great favourite with the men.
Catherine Oh dear! How can you say so?
Isabella I know you very well. You have so much animation, which is exactly what Miss Andrews lacks, for I must confess, there is something amazingly insipid about her; but I see how it is, you are indifferent to everybody's admiration, except that of one gentleman, who shall be nameless ...

Scene 13

The Play Begins

The house Lights of the onstage theatre go down. In the background, two sixteenth-century figures (actually the actors who play James Morland and John Thorpe) appear and embark on a violent altercation

Isabella and Catherine pay only a little attention

First Actor This also shall not pass unnoticed. I bid you learn, sir, that you have a stronger enemy than a woman to contend with. You have misled me, and would revenge your disappointed views upon the innocent!
Isabella (*sotto voce, world-weary*) Ah men! They give themselves such airs. They are the most conceited creatures in the world, and think themselves of such importance ...

There are cries of "Shhh!" from other members of the audience

Second Actor Count Morano! This is the language and conduct of a passionate *boy*, and as such I pass over it in contempt!
Isabella (*as the play mutters on in the background*) By the bye — what is your favourite complexion in a man? Do you like them best dark or fair?
Catherine I hardly know. Something between both, I think. Brown, not fair, and not very dark ...
Isabella I have not forgot your description of Mr Tilney: "A brown skin, with dark eyes, and rather dark hair." Well, my taste is different!
First Actor (*furiously*) Draw! This in thy heart, villain! They shall carry you from Udolpho in your coffin!

And a fight proceeds, largely ignored by Isabella and Catherine

Isabella (*musing*) I prefer light eyes, and as to complexion: do you know, I like a sallow better than any other? Rather like your brother's. Now you must not betray me, if you should ever meet with one of your acquaintance answering that description.
Catherine (*confused*) Betray you! What do you mean?
Second Actor Betray you? What do you mean?

Catherine is startled by this coincidence of expression

Isabella Nay, do not distress me. I believe I have said too much. Let us drop the subject. (*She sighs*)

During the following speech the actor becomes louder and the girls pay attention

Second Actor You are a villain! If there is treachery in this affair, look to yourself as the author of it. But why do I use words? Come on, coward, and receive justice at my hands!

The first actor rushes after the second and they fight, the fight raging around the two terrified girls, who cower below the combatants

Act I, Scene 14

There is the sudden blast of a post horn. They all freeze

Scene 14

James and John

During the following narration, the two actors have their cloaks and masks removed, and stand revealed as James Morland and John Thorpe

Dimity (*to the audience*) Two days later, at the junction of Union Passage and Cheap Street, Isabella and Catherine were prevented from crossing by the approach of a gig, driven by a most knowing-looking coachman with all the vehemence that could most fitly endanger the lives of himself, his companion, and his horse.

The Lights switch. Daytime. Street noise. Horses whinnying

John Upon my soul!
Isabella (*ecstatically*) Oh delightful! Mr Morland and my brother!
Catherine Good heavens! 'Tis James!
James Catherine! Why, this is fortunate! How smart you look. I hardly know you. Thorpe, let me introduce you to my sister.
John (*with his best stab at charm*) Your very attentive and obedient, madam!
James (*blushing*) Miss Thorpe ... I had not expected ... How long it seems since ... When we last met ... That is, your brother told me you were ...
Catherine James! You did not write to tell me you were coming. Is not Mama expecting you at home? Why have you changed your plans?
Isabella (*quickly, smoothly*) To give his sister a surprise. I conjured him for you, and he appeared.
Catherine You dear old thing. To come this far for me. (*The slightest hint of a beat*) Oh, Mr Thorpe, your sister and I are now the closest friends.
Isabella You look well, brother.
John And you look very ugly, Belle.
Catherine (*horrified*) Mr Thorpe!
James Take no notice of him, Kate, it is his way. He is as good-natured a fellow as ever lived. A little of a rattle — but that will recommend him to your sex, I believe.
John Miss Morland, may I have the first dance with you tonight? You will be visiting the Upper Rooms?

Isabella draws John away

Isabella You donkey! Miss Morland may have other offers.

John She can cancel 'em.
James (*aside, to Catherine*) How do you like my friend Thorpe?
Catherine I do not — know. He seems so ...
James And Isabella?
Catherine (*warmly*) Very very much.
James She has so much good sense, and is so thoroughly unaffected and amiable. I always wanted you to know her.
Catherine I love her exceedingly. But you hardly mentioned her after your visit there ...
James (*not hearing her*) I need not ask you whether you are happy here. With such a companion and friend as Isabella Thorpe, it would be impossible for you to be otherwise.
Catherine How good it is of you to come so far on purpose to see me.
James (*and it is no less the truth*) Indeed, Catherine, I love you dearly.

Isabella and John return

John Morland! You see my sister to her lodgings, I'll escort Miss Morland back to hers.
Isabella (*whispering in Catherine's ear*) My brother thinks you the most charming girl in the world!

Scene 15

John Talks

And James whirls Isabella away

John and Catherine set out to walk home

John How long do you think we have been running it from Tetbury, Miss Morland? Five and twenty miles if it is an inch. I know it must be five and twenty by the time we have been doing it. It is now half-past one. We drove out of the inn yard at Tetbury as the town clock struck eleven, and I defy any man in England to make my horse go less than ten miles an hour in harness. That makes it exactly twenty-five.

Mrs Thorpe appears

Mrs Thorpe (*to the audience*) They came upon Mrs Thorpe at the corner of Cheap Street.
John Ah, Mother! How do you do? Where did you get that quiz of a hat, it makes you look like an old witch! I shall be with you shortly. Miss Morland

Act I, Scene 16   21

here has promised me her first dance tonight. (*To Catherine*) What did you think of my gig, Miss Morland? A neat one, is it not? Well hung, town built. I have not had it a month. It was built for a Christchurch man, a friend of mine, a very good sort of fellow. "Ah! Thorpe!" says he. "Do you happen to want such a little thing as this? It is a capital thing of its kind, but I am cursed tired of it." "Oh damn," said I, "I am your man, what do you ask?" And how much do you think he did, Miss Morland ...?

Catherine, unable to speak, steps into the arms of Mrs Allen and into her ball gown for the night. John moves away, returning to the women as Mrs Allen's following speech ends

Mrs Allen (*to the audience*) Thorpe deposited Catherine at Pulteney Street, but returned in good time that evening to escort Mrs Allen and her young companion to the ball.
John How much do you think he asked for it? Remember: curricle-hung; seat, trunk, sword-case, splashing board, lamps, silver moulding, all complete. The iron-work is as good as new or better. He asked fifty guineas! I closed with him directly, threw down the money, and the carriage was mine. I might have got it for less, I dare say, but I hate haggling.

A chandelier descends. The Lights change and music begins

The Upper Rooms

Five chairs are set up, facing alternately up and down stage, giving an indication of the seating for the ball

(*Continuing, regardless*) Now don't forget, Miss Morland, that your first dance this evening is with John Thorpe! But if you'll excuse me, I must just now go into the card room to speak with a friend. Remember! Your first dance!

SCENE 16

Adrift at the Ball

And John vanishes, leaving Catherine with Isabella, James and Mrs Allen

James (*excitedly*) Come, Miss Thorpe; the first dance is about to begin. Why do we delay?
Isabella (*adamant*) I assure you, I have vowed not to begin without your dear

sister. We might be separated the whole evening.

James whispers to Isabella during the following

Mrs Allen (*to anyone who will listen*) I have never been in such a fret. The satin draperies above the trim were still unstitched at twenty after five. Never have I known a dressmaker so slow ...
Catherine (*supportively*) But the effect, Mrs Allen, is uncommonly tasteful. And striking.
Mrs Allen I think it has already caused a stir.
James (*the end of his whispered plea*) — I know she will not mind it ...

Music is heard

Isabella (*to Catherine*) My dear creature, I am afraid I must leave you; your brother is impatient to begin. I know you will not mind my going, and I daresay John will be back in a moment!

Isabella and James dance

Catherine Oh, where is Mr Thorpe? People will think I do not have a partner, like all the other ladies sitting down!
Mrs Allen Be patient, my dear.

Suddenly, Mr Tilney is there — with a new young lady, Eleanor Tilney, a kind, attentive, pretty girl. Catherine sits up

Tilney Good-evening, Mrs Allen.
Mrs Allen Mr Tilney!
Tilney May I introduce my sister. Mrs Allen, Miss Morland: this is Eleanor Tilney.
Mrs Allen My dear, how charming. Please sit here by me. Well, Mr Tilney, I am very happy to see you again; indeed I was afraid you had left Bath.
Tilney Affairs in Gloucestershire called me home for a week.
Mrs Allen Well sir, and I daresay you are not sorry to be back again, for it is just the place for young people — and indeed for everyone else, too. Miss Tilney, I tell Mr Allen...

And the conversation between Mrs Allen and Eleanor fades away from us

Tilney Miss Morland.
Catherine Oh, Mr Tilney, I am so pleased to see you again.
Tilney I hope you have forgiven me.

Act I, Scene 16   23

Catherine For what?
Tilney Detaining you a week ago, or leaving town, or coming back again. I cannot quite decide.
Catherine (*laughing*) You are forgiven!
Tilney And will you dance with me?
Catherine Oh yes ... That is ... Oh. No...
Mrs Allen (*turning back from talking to Miss Tilney*) Remember, Catherine, you have promised Thorpe your first dance...
Catherine (*somewhat too apologetically*) Now it is you who must forgive me, Mr Tilney! I am so sorry. Indeed I did not know that I should see you here. If I had known ——
John (*from a distance*) Miss Morland! (*He heads for Catherine*)
Tilney Your partner?

Catherine is distraught

Mrs Allen (*unhelpfully*) Mr Tilney, will you walk with me a little?

Tilney and Mrs Allen withdraw

John (*arriving*) Miss Morland, I have kept you waiting a while, but with good reason. I have been with Clay, a splendid fellow, Christchurch man, keeps a full stable. Promised me a ride on Valiant, a creature made for speed, forehand of a champion, loins like a tiger; there is not a horse like him in England ... Now, Clay has a fancy to exchange one of my terriers — a wire-haired — for one of *his* — a smooth — and I must leave you for another minute. Jackson over there will know the pedigree. Clay's pack is famous, and if Old King Pippin is the sire ...

And he is gone again

Catherine is left with Eleanor

Eleanor (*after a moment*) Do you like Bath?
Catherine Oh, very much.

A beat

Eleanor The Paragon is quite the finest and most elegant of buildings.
Catherine I like the Abbey. It reminds me of the monastery in *Udolpho* ... (*Suddenly, she sees something and stops*) Who is your brother dancing with?
Eleanor I think that is Miss Smith.

A longish beat

Catherine (*recovering her concentration*) Do you draw?
Eleanor A little. For my own pleasure. Do you?
Catherine No. Well. When I must.
Eleanor And do you play?

A beat

Catherine No. Well. Very badly.
Eleanor Henry has told me that you dance ——
Catherine Yes?
Eleanor Delightfully.
Catherine He has spoken of me, then?

Mrs Allen returns. She takes Eleanor away during the following

Mrs Allen Miss Tilney! I am sent to take you to your brother. He has found Miss Hughes and Mr Wallace, and they will not rest till they have fixed a time to see your drawings of the town, which Mr Tilney swears are quite the most accomplished ...

And they are gone

Catherine is left alone. She looks around

Suddenly, James and Isabella return

Isabella At *last* I have got you. My dearest creature, I have been looking for you this hour.
Catherine I have been here all the time.
Isabella So I told your brother, but he would not believe me.
James (*protesting*) Unjust!
Isabella *Was it not so*, Mr Morland?
Catherine You see the young lady over there with Mrs Allen? It is Mr Tilney's sister!
Isabella (*gasping*) What a delightful girl!

Music begins again

But where is her all-conquering brother? I die to see him.
James The music is begun. The *Allemande*! Come ...
Isabella I would not do such a thing!
James No one will mind!

And Isabella and James dash off. A few more beats

Act I, Scene 16

John returns, slumping next to Catherine

John Gone! Jackson has left. I could not find the fellow.

A long moment. Catherine screws her courage up and tries to chat

Catherine Do you read at all, Mr Thorpe?
John (*disgruntled*) As little as possible.
Catherine Have you ever read *Udolpho*, Mr Thorpe?
John *Udolpho*? Oh Lord! Not I; I never read novels. Novels are all so full of stuff and nonsense; they are the stupidest things in creation.
Catherine I think you must like *Udolpho*, if you were to read it. It is so very interesting.
John Not I, faith! No, if I read any, it shall be one of Mrs Radcliffe's; her novels are amusing enough.
Catherine (*after a beat*) *Udolpho* was written by Mrs Radcliffe.
John No? Was it? Yes, of course, yes, so it was. I was thinking of that other stupid book.
Catherine (*after a beat*) Ah.

Mrs Allen returns and sits, puffed

Mrs Allen My dear, Mrs Thorpe has told me a great deal about the Tilneys!
Catherine What did she tell you?
Mrs Allen Oh, a vast deal indeed, but I cannot recollect it now. But they are a very good kind of people, and very rich.
Catherine And are their parents in Bath?
Mrs Allen Yes, yes, I fancy they are, but I am not quite certain. Upon recollection, however, I have a notion they are both dead ... At least the mother is. I think the father is a general — YES! He is a general and alive! We shall see him at the Cotillion Ball!

Eleanor Tilney appears

Catherine (*jumping up*) Miss Tilney. How well your brother dances!
Eleanor Henry! Yes, he does dance very well.
Catherine He must have thought it very odd to hear me say earlier that I was engaged, when he has seen me sitting down the whole evening. But I really was engaged to Mr Thorpe. You cannot think how surprised I was to see your brother again. I felt sure of his being quite gone away. Who was that young lady?
Eleanor Miss Smith?
Catherine I dare say she was very glad to dance. Do you think her pretty?
Eleanor Not very.

Catherine Might he visit the Pump Room tomorrow?
Eleanor Very possibly. Shall we meet you there?
Catherine (*brightening*) I should like nothing better ——
John (*suddenly*) You have not forgot *our* engagement? Did we not agree together to take a drive tomorrow morning? What a head you have! We are going up Claverton Down.
Catherine (*faintly*) Oh no.
Eleanor It does not matter in the least. Another day, perhaps. Good-night Miss Morland, Mrs Allen.
Catherine (*a despairing appeal; to Mrs Allen*) Claverton Down!
Mrs Allen (*misinterpreting*) Of *course* you may. Do *just* as you please, my dear.

SCENE 17

The Curricle Ride

Music

The scene quickly changes to: the carriage. John helps Catherine in, also helping her into a day bonnet etc. He is given a whip and reins

John Do not be frightened, Miss Morland, if my horse should dance about a little at first. He will, most likely, give a plunge or two, but he will know his master. He is full of spirits, playful as can be. Very well! (*To a servant*) LET HIM GO!

Very *gentle trotting noises. A moment or two passes*

Catherine (*hugely relieved*) But he moves very gently!
John If the reins are held just so, and then you crack the whip at every seventh stride, just a little behind his left ear ... (*He demonstrates*)

The horse's hooves speed up for a moment, but subside again to a slow clip-clop

Catherine Indeed, Mr Thorpe, you have a perfect command of him.
John (*after a beat: wheedling, greedy*) Old Allen is as rich as Croesus, is he not?
Catherine I beg your pardon?
John Old Allen. Mrs Allen's husband.
Catherine Oh! Mr Allen. Yes, I believe he is very rich.
John And no children at all?

Act I, Scene 17   27

Catherine Not any.
John A famous thing for his next heirs. He *is* your godfather, is he not?
Catherine My godfather? No!
John But you are always very much with them.
Catherine Yes, very much.
John Ah. Good. (*He gestures to either side with his riding crop*) Everywhere you look — women! Look there! Beta minus! Over here: gamma plus. (*Beat. He jabs at a passer-by with his riding crop; tolerantly*) Beta plus. (*He does it again; approvingly*) And alpha minus ... Beta ... Gamma ... Beta... (*He stands up in his seat*) OMEGA! (*He laughs mightily at this*)

Thorpe's laughter rumbles on through the following interchange during which the horse, inspired by its master's enthusiasm, gets faster and faster

Catherine (*to the audience*) Catherine could not entirely repress a doubt ——

Tilney appears at the roadside

Tilney — while she bore with the effusions of his endless conceit ——
Catherine — of whether or not he was altogether agreeable. He told her of horses he had bought for a trifle ——
John *Ten shillings*!
Catherine — and sold for incredible sums ——
John A *hundred* guineas!
Catherine — of racing matches ——
John Forty to one...
Catherine — in which his judgement had infallibly foretold the winner ——
John Only had a shilling on her, though ...
Catherine — of shooting parties ——
John (*startlingly*) Boom-boom!
Catherine —in which he killed more birds ——
John And not one good shot!
Catherine — than all his companions together!
John Fifty-two brace!
Catherine And a famous hunt, in which his foresight and skill in directing the dogs ——
John Whip 'em till they *squeal*...
Catherine — had repaired the mistakes of the most experienced huntsman ——
John Old nut-head!

Catherine — and in which the boldness of his riding had constantly led others into danger!
John (*delightedly*) Three of them broke their damned necks!

Scene 18

Catherine Won't Dance

Chandeliers, music, candlelight

The last stage of a Cotillion dance, involving Isabella and James and Mrs Allen and General Tilney and Miss Tilney. The fourth set piece [See Music Plot]. Catherine, having extricated herself from the clutches of John Thorpe, avoids him as he looks for her among the dancers. The dance ends

Catherine (*to the audience*) On the evening of the Cotillion Ball, Catherine was chiefly anxious to avoid John Thorpe, lest he should engage her again; for though she could not, *dared* not expect that Mr Tilney should ask her a third time to dance, her wishes, hopes and plans all centred on nothing less ... (*To Isabella*) Miss Tilney said he would be here.
Isabella Do not be frightened, my dear Catherine, but I am really going to dance with your brother again ——
Catherine The Cotillions are over, the country dances have begun — and still no sign of him.
Isabella I declare positively it is quite shocking. I tell your brother he ought to be ashamed of himself.
Catherine I will not dance until I dance with Mr Tilney.
Isabella Oh, dance with my brother, dear Catherine. He is desperate and longs to be your partner.
Catherine I cannot. What would Mr Tilney think?
Isabella Where *is* Mr Tilney? Are you promised to him?
Catherine I am promised to no-one.
Isabella But you lay traps for everyone. You will not be content until the last gentleman in Bath is out of sorts on your account. What games you play.

John Thorpe rolls up. Out of sorts

John Heyday, Miss Morland! What is the meaning of this? I thought you and I were to dance together.
Isabella Why should she want to dance with you, mooncalf? Miss Morland hasn't come here to be *muddied* ...
John (*warningly*) Belle ...
Catherine I wonder you should think so, Mr Thorpe, for you never asked me.

John That is a good one, by Jove! I asked you as soon as I came into the room!
Isabella You asked for a glass of wine when you first came into the room ——
John And I was just going to ask you again, but when I turned round, you were gone! This is a cursed shabby trick!
Catherine I never told you I would dance with you tonight, Mr Thorpe.
John I only came for the sake of dancing with you. And I have been telling all my acquaintance here that I was going to dance with the prettiest girl in the room...
Catherine Well then, they will never think you mean *me* ——
John By heavens, if they do not, I will kick them out of the room for blockheads!

SCENE 19

General Tilney

Tilney arrives with an older man, General Tilney, who is dark, vigorous, beetle-browed

The others fall silent

Tilney Miss Morland, good-evening. I should like you to meet my father, General Tilney.
General (*unexpectedly gracious*) I am delighted to make your acquaintance, Miss Morland. My son has spoken of you. We are a little late. I hope you are not inconvenienced in any way. Our coachman is the dullest fellow. Of course, you will sit with us tonight. We have a table in the Persian room. My daughter Eleanor is there. I trust that your companions here will not refuse to spare you to her.
Isabella (*impressed*) No!
John (*very impressed*) Not at all!
Catherine (*relieved*) Why no, I am sure they will have the least objection...
John (*pushing forward*) General Tilney. My friend Miss Morland would be honoured and delighted to sit with you tonight.
General (*gruffly*) I'm glad to hear it.
John Thorpe. John Thorpe. It is a rare honour and privilege to salute you. Perhaps you recall our meeting at the Bedford last October...?
General Perhaps I do.
Catherine (*hastily*) General Tilney, Mr Tilney; this is my very dear friend, Miss Thorpe.
General Yes, yes.

Tilney Your servant, Miss Thorpe.

Music starts again

General There! The Scottish reel. You young people had best dance!
Tilney Miss Morland?
Catherine (*delightedly*) Yes! Oh yes...

And Henry and Catherine retreat to await the beginning of the next reel with James, Isabella, Mrs Allen and Eleanor Tilney

General You know Miss Morland?
John (*overwhelmed at the General's interest*) Oh yes, why yes! A dear friend. And I hope one day...
General A good family?
John The best, the very best! Old Mr Morland — very well set up. My own family would view an alliance there ——
General Who's the old lady, her companion?
John Allen, Mrs Allen. Devoted to her. And Mr Allen too. One of the richest men in Wiltshire. Countless acres. Farms, estates, grazing, a dozen villages, three hunts ——
General (*suddenly*) Billiards!
John Billiards?
General We've time for half a game. Come.
John (*bursting with pride*) At once.

SCENE 20

Henry and Catherine Dance

The dancers take up their positions. The following dialogue is spoken during the dance, which is the fifth set piece [See Music Plot]

Tilney Mr Thorpe seems most concerned for you.
Catherine He means well.
Tilney He would have put me out of patience had he intervened again on your behalf. He has no business to withdraw the attention of my partner from me. I consider a country dance as an emblem of marriage. Those men who do not choose to dance or marry themselves, have no business with the partners or wives of their neighbours.
Catherine But they are such very different things!
Tilney That you think they cannot be compared together.

Catherine People that marry can never part. People that dance only stand opposite each other in a long room for half an hour.
Tilney So if Mr Thorpe were to return, there would be nothing to restrain you from conversing with him for as long as you chose?
Catherine Mr Thorpe is a special friend of my brother's. If he talks to me, I must talk to him. But there are hardly three young men in the room beside him that I have any acquaintance with.
Tilney And is that to be my only security? Alas, alas!
Catherine You cannot have a better: for if I do not know anybody, it is impossible for me to talk to them; and besides, I do not *want* to talk to anybody.
Tilney Now you have given me a security worth having ...

The dance finishes. Tilney and Catherine promenade

Do you find Bath as agreeable as you did before?
Catherine Yes, quite — more so, indeed.
Tilney But Bath compared with London has little variety. And so everybody finds out every year.
Catherine But I, who live in a small retired village in the country, must always find a greater variety here in Bath than in my own home. If I could but have Mama and Papa and the rest of them here, I suppose I should be too happy. Oh, who can ever be tired of Bath?
Tilney (*genuinely impressed*) Not those who bring such fresh feelings of every sort to it as you do!

Scene 21

The General's Invitation

General Tilney and John reappear

General Miss Morland! Is your dancing finished?
Catherine For the moment, General Tilney.
General I approve the way you dance. Spirited and bold. It finds an echo in your walk. I commend the elasticity of your walk. You move well, Miss Morland!
John I have a horse the very same. A famous clever animal for the road; only forty guineas. I ——
General (*cutting across*) Miss Morland, we take a picnic to Beechen Cliff tomorrow at twelve. Will you join us? It promises to be a fine day.
John Nothing could give us greater pleasure.

General (*very firmly*) But you were telling me you planned a drive to Clifton in the morning, Mr Thorpe. I do not think you will be back for lunch. Shall we call for you, Miss Morland?
Catherine Mr and Mrs Allen can have no objection. I shall go and ask them now.
General Splendid. And then, please join us at our table. My daughter is anxious to speak with you again. Come Henry.

SCENE 22

John Knows the General

Tilney and the General move away

John and Catherine are left alone together

John (*after a moment*) He is a fine old fellow, upon my soul! I have a great regard for him.
Catherine (*puzzled*) But how came you to know him?

During the following, Catherine slips away

John (*airily*) There are few people much about town that I do not know. We set to at billiards just now. He is good. One of the best players we have, by the bye. The odds were five to four against me. And if I had not made one of the cleanest strokes that perhaps ever was made… (*He looks around and notices that Catherine has slipped away. He smiles roguishly: perhaps she is playing "hard to get"*) Damn me! *Gone!*

John exits in pursuit of Catherine

SCENE 23

Dissent

Catherine's lodgings, the next day. The sounds of hooves and carriages in the next street outside. Jolly, "off for a good day out" music

Catherine (*to the audience*) The following morning, at a quarter before twelve ——
John Make haste! Make haste! Put on your hat this moment; there is no time to be lost, we are going to Bristol!
Catherine You know I cannot go with you today!

Act I, Scene 23   33

Nobody listens to Catherine

Isabella We shall have a most heavenly drive. You are to thank your brother and me for the scheme. We planned it last night after the country dancing. I am in such ecstasies at the thought of a little country air and quiet!
Catherine I cannot go. I expect General Tilney to call on me at twelve. We have an expedition planned ...
John We shall drive directly to Clifton and dine there, and as soon as dinner is over go on to Kingsweston!
James I doubt our being able to do so much.
John You croaking fellow! We shall be able to do ten times more. Kingsweston, aye, and Blaize Castle too...
Catherine (*taken by the name*) Blaize Castle! Oh, I should like to see that — but I cannot, *cannot* go.

They hear her for the first time. There is a beat

Isabella Cannot? Why?
Catherine I have settled with the Tilneys to walk to Beechen Cliff.
Isabella Retract!
The Men Retract!
Isabella We will not go without you!
James It is nothing to put off a mere walk...
Isabella We will not hear of a refusal!
Catherine Do not urge me, Isabella. I am engaged to the Tilneys. I cannot go with you.
Isabella (*sweetly*) Dear Catherine, it would be so easy to tell the Tilneys that you had just been reminded of a prior engagement, and must only beg to put off the walk until Tuesday.
Catherine No, it would not be easy. I could not do it. There has been no prior engagement.
Isabella (*very sweetly and firmly*) Dearest, sweetest Catherine! Please, please go with us. You will not seriously refuse so trifling a request. I know you have too feeling a heart, too sweet a temper not to be persuaded by those who love you.
Catherine You must forgive me Isabella. (*An attempt at imparting a confidence*) This is an invitation from the Tilneys. The first indication, the first sign perhaps ——
Isabella (*suddenly very sharp*) I cannot help being jealous, Catherine, when I see myself slighted for strangers — *I* , who love you so excessively! I believe my feelings are stronger than anybody's; I am sure they are too strong for my own peace. And to see myself supplanted in your friendship by strangers does cut me to the quick, I own. These Tilneys seem to swallow up everything else.

Catherine Go without me!
John I did not come to Bath to drive my sister about, and look like a fool. No. If you do not go, damn me if I do!

A very awkward few moments pass. Catherine looks to her brother for support

James (*reproachfully*) I did not think you had been so obstinate, Catherine. You were not used to be so hard to persuade; you once were the kindest, best tempered of sisters …
Catherine I hope I am not less so now, but indeed I cannot go. If I am wrong, I am doing what I believe to be right.
Isabella (*in a low voice*) I suspect there is no great struggle.

There is another difficult moment. Then John starts to laugh

Isabella John!
John (*brightly*) But no need to quarrel. I have already settled the matter, and you may come with a safe conscience. (*Beat*) I called on General Tilney early this morning. Told him that you had quite resolved to come with us to Clifton, and that you would not have the pleasure of walking with them until tomorrow. He did not in the least seem to mind.
Catherine You have done WHAT?

Music. Suddenly, John metamorphoses into a cloaked villain from Udolpho, *and grabs Catherine*

Villain I have made your excuses. He said tomorrow they might undertake another trip. So there is an end to our difficulties. So now you may come with us to* Udolpho*!

Tilney appears as a "romantic hero"

Catherine (*struggling*) It was all a mistake; I never promised to go, I told them from the first I could not go. I cannot imagine what you think of me; Mr Thorpe never told me he would call upon you …
Tilney Begone, you devil!

A struggle; Catherine is released

We hear the Abbey bell ring twelve. Meanwhile, we see General Tilney and his children assemble for the outing

Act I, Scene 24   35

(*To the audience; as himself*) Catherine arrived a few moments before the Tilneys were due to leave.
Eleanor (*to the audience*) She found that John Thorpe *had* given the message ——
General (*to the audience*) — and General Tilney had no scruple in owning himself greatly surprised by it.
Eleanor (*placatingly*) Whatever might have been felt *before* her arrival, her eager declarations immediately made every look and sentence as friendly as she could desire.
General (*turning to Catherine, welcoming her*) Miss Morland.
Tilney (*to the audience*) The party set out for Beechen Cliff.

SCENE 24

Beechen Cliff

A scene of picturesque loveliness. Deep golden sunshine, a glimpse of an old ruin, a picnic. Music: an expansive "noble" theme

Catherine (*enraptured*) It is so beautiful here! I never look at it without thinking of the south of France.
General (*surprised*) You have been abroad then?
Catherine Oh! No. I only mean what I have read about. It always puts me in mind of the country that Emily and her father travelled through in *The Mysteries of Udolpho*. But you never read novels, I dare say?
Tilney Why not?
Catherine Because they are not clever enough for you. Gentlemen read better books.
General (*humorously*) True enough!
Tilney (*tongue-in-cheek*) The person, be it gentleman or lady, who has not pleasure in a good novel must be intolerably stupid. *The Mysteries of Udolpho*, when I had once begun it, I could not lay down again. I remember finishing it in two days, my hair standing on end the whole time. I am proud when I reflect upon it. And think it must establish me in your good opinion.
Catherine I am very glad to hear it indeed, and now I shall never be ashamed of liking *Udolpho* myself.
Eleanor You are fond of that kind of reading?
Catherine To say the truth, I do not much like any other.
Eleanor Indeed!
Catherine That is, I can read poetry and plays and things of that sort, and do not dislike travels. But history, for example, real solemn history, I cannot be interested in. Can you?

Eleanor Yes, I am fond of history.
Catherine I wish I were too. I read it a little as a duty, but it tells me nothing that does not either vex or weary me. The quarrels of popes and kings, with wars or pestilences in every page; the men all so good for nothing, and hardly any women at all — it is very tiresome. Whereas Mrs Radcliffe ——
Eleanor How do you suppose she would have written of this view before us, Miss Morland?
Catherine (*at a loss*) Well. I hardly know. She might have mentioned the town, and perhaps the blue of the sky and the hills over there ...
Tilney She would write of it as we might paint the picture.
Catherine (*enthused*) Yes, oh yes — the rows of houses and the Abbey and the crescent ——
Tilney Do you draw, Miss Morland?
Catherine (*abashed*) Hardly at all. I know so little about it. I would give anything in the world to be able to draw.
Tilney You might begin by composing your picture. In the foreground you could place my sister, or my father, reading there. Behind and to the left, a sidescreen: that single oak perhaps, to make the first stage of the perspective. In the immediate distance, my subject might comprise that ruined tower and the wooded hill on which it sits. The second distance — scarcely seen, between those avenues of trees — might just include a glimpse of streets and houses. Our inspiration should not be the town seen *thus*, but we should frame our picture to suggest the *possibility* of Bath. Judicious obscurity is all the fashion now.

A beat

General (*suddenly*) I daresay Mr Allen's great estates are full of views. Wiltshire is pretty is it not? And prosperous.
Catherine It is. And I think that if I saw it again today and had your son to guide me it might seem twice as beautiful as when I saw it last ...
General You are a lucky girl, Miss Morland. One of the luckiest in Bath, I dare say.

A beat. Eleanor and Tilney exchange looks: what's his drift? Catherine is encouraged

Catherine (*solemnly*) I have heard that something very shocking indeed will soon come out in London.
Eleanor (*with concern*) Indeed! And of what nature?
Catherine That I do not know, nor who is the author. I have only heard that it is to be more horrible than anything we have met with yet.

Act I, Scene 25   37

Eleanor (*worriedly*) Good heaven! Where could you hear of such a thing?
Catherine A particular friend of mine had an account of it in a letter from London yesterday. It is to be uncommonly dreadful. I shall expect murder, and everything of the kind!
Eleanor You speak with astonishing composure! But I hope your friend's accounts have been exaggerated; and if such a design is known beforehand, proper measures will undoubtedly be taken by government to prevent its coming to effect.
Catherine By government?
Tilney There must be murder — and government cares not how much.
Eleanor But have the goodness to satisfy me as to the cause of this dreadful riot!
Catherine Riot! What riot?
Tilney (*vastly amused*) Eleanor, the riot is only in your brain! Do you understand? Miss Morland, you spoke of expected horrors in London, and instead of instantly conceiving, as any rational creature would have done, that you were speaking of a *book*, my sister immediately pictured to herself a mob of three thousand men, the Bank attacked, the Tower threatened, the streets of London flowing with blood, and our brother — the gallant Captain Frederick Tilney — knocked off his horse by a brickbat from an upper window. (*A beat*) Forgive her stupidity, but she is by no means a simpleton in general...
Eleanor Henry! Do you mean to have Miss Morland think you intolerably rude to your sister, and a great brute in general? She is not used to your odd ways.
Tilney I shall be most happy to make her better acquainted with them.

The next scene begins to overwhelm the end of this one. Isabella approaches holding a note

Isabella Catherine! Catherine!
Eleanor We shall get nothing more serious from him now, Miss Morland. He is not in a sober mood ...
Isabella (*insistently*) My dearest Kate!
Eleanor But it would be hard for him to say a truly unjust thing of any woman ——
Isabella (*to the audience*) Early the next day...
Eleanor — or an unkind one of me.

SCENE 25

Isabella's News

Isabella triumphs. The previous scene has to retreat. The Tilneys go

Isabella (*handing Catherine the note*) A note from Isabella, speaking peace and tenderness in every line — and entreating the immediate presence of her friend on a matter of the utmost importance ——
Catherine You went to Clifton!
Isabella Yes.
Catherine With James …
Isabella Yes, my dear Catherine, it is so indeed. Your penetration has not deceived you. Oh that arch eye of yours! It sees through everything.
Catherine (*thoroughly baffled*) Indeed?
Isabella Nay, my beloved, sweetest friend; compose yourself. I am amazingly agitated as you perceive. *Sly* creature! Oh! my dear Catherine, you alone who know my heart can judge of my present happiness.
Catherine I can?
Isabella Your brother is the most charming of men…
Catherine (*genuinely at a loss*) James?
Isabella I only wish I was more worthy of him. But what will your excellent father and mother say? Oh! heavens when I think of them, I am so agitated!
Catherine My dear Isabella, what *do you mean*? Can you really be in love with James?
Isabella (*nodding excitedly*) *And yesterday*, three and a half miles outside Kingsweston, Mr Morland made a tender and passionate confession of his love for me!

Catherine gives a squeal of delight

You will be so infinitely dearer to me, my Catherine, than my own brothers and sisters. I feel that I shall be so much more attached to my dear Morland's family than to my own.
Catherine (*amazed; then, to the audience*) This was a pitch of friendship beyond Catherine.
Isabella The very first day that Morland came to us last Christmas, the very moment I beheld him, my heart was irrevocably gone. I remember I wore my yellow gown, with my hair done up in braids; and when I came into the drawing room, I thought I had never seen anybody so handsome before.
Catherine (*incredulous*) James?
Isabella Here he is!

James enters, wrapped up for a ride and clutching bags. John Thorpe is just behind him

I have told Catherine *everything!*
James Dearest Catherine: I leave for Fullerton this instant to make known the happy news and seek our father's consent.

Isabella My fortune will be so small. They never can consent to it.
John Oh stuff!
Catherine You are too humble. The difference of fortune can be *nothing!*
James I have no doubt of our parents giving their consent immediately.
John Stupid girl.
Isabella I only wish our situations were reversed. Had I the command of millions, were I mistress of the whole world, your brother would be my only choice.

And James and Isabella hold hands

Catherine (*to the audience*) This charming sentiment gave Catherine a most pleasing remembrance of all the heroines of her acquaintance, and she thought her friend never looked more lovely than in uttering this grand idea.

The two lovers rush out

SCENE 26

John Gets Romantic

Catherine is left with John. Again

John A famous good thing this marrying scheme, upon my soul! A clever fancy of Morland's and Belle's. What do you think of it, Miss Morland? I say it is no bad notion.
Catherine I am sure that I think it is a very good one.
John Do you? That's honest, by heavens. I am glad you are no enemy to matrimony. (*A beat*) Did you ever hear the old song: "Going to one wedding brings on another"? Well. Perhaps we may try the truth of this same old song.
Catherine (*adrift*) May we? But I never sing. Well. I wish you a very good afternoon — I must be going home.
John Nay — but there is no such confounded hurry!
Catherine No?
John Upon my soul: I do not know anybody like you!
Catherine Oh! Dear… There are a great many people like me, I dare say, only a great deal better.
John But I say, Miss Morland, I shall come and pay my respects at Fullerton before too long, if not disagreeable.
Catherine Pray do. My father and mother will be very glad to see you.
John And I hope … I hope, Miss Morland, *you* will not be sorry to see me.

Catherine Oh dear! Not at all. There are very few people I am sorry to see. Company is always cheerful. Good-day!

And she rushes out

John (*smiling cheerfully; to the audience*) My notion of things is simple enough. Let me only have the girl I like, say I, with a comfortable house over my head, and what care I for another thing? Fortune is nothing. Let me only have the company of the people I love, let me only be where I like and with whom I like, and the devil take the rest.

And he stomps off happily enough

SCENE 27

Good News

A sudden shriek. Isabella comes running on with Catherine; James appears in another part of the stage

James Dearest Isabella ...
Isabella His letter! Catherine, his LETTER! I cannot, *cannot* read it. I know it is bad news. You must read it to me. Oh Catherine, Catherine ...
James Dearest Isabella ——
Catherine I am sure my parents will be delighted with you!
Isabella Here, *here*!
James Dearest Isabella ——
Catherine Very well, very well ... let me see ... ah, yes, it is from James — yes. He begins: "Dearest Isabella —— "
James (*taking over*) I have had no difficulty in gaining the consent of my kind parents, and am promised that everything in their power shall be done to forward my happiness ——

Catherine and Isabella squawk and crow with delight, hug, kiss, dance, cry etc.

(*Trying to continue*) — it will be another day perhaps ——
Isabella Isabella knew enough ——
James — before they can resolve how our income is to be formed ——
Isabella — to feel secure of an honourable and speedy establishment.
James — some small parcel of landed property may be resigned to us ——
Isabella (*who does not want to hear about details*) She saw herself at the end of a few weeks, the gaze and admiration of every new acquaintance ——

James — or perhaps some funded money could be made available. I fear it will not make us rich ——
Isabella — with a carriage at her command, a new name on her calling card, and a brilliant exhibition of hooped rings on her finger!

Scene 28

The Tilneys Preoccupied

Isabella dances off round the stage. The Tilneys drift by

Catherine (*to the audience*) That evening at the Upper Rooms, Catherine was met by the General with true kindness ...
General The happiest part of our residence in Bath has been the accident of meeting you, Miss Morland.
Eleanor While Miss Tilney took pains to be near her ——
Tilney — and Henry asked her to dance.

Isabella returns

Isabella I fear I shall not be very agreeable this evening, for my heart, you know, is some forty miles off. And as for dancing: do not mention it, I beg; it is quite out of the question.

Scene 29

Captain Tilney

A sudden chord marks the appearance of Captain Tilney, a very fashionable, handsome young man in smart military uniform. The Tilneys move to greet him

Isabella Oh. Who is that?
Catherine I think it is the elder brother — Captain Tilney.
Isabella Oh.
Catherine Captain Frederick Tilney.
Isabella Oh.
Catherine He is indeed a handsome gentleman.
Isabella Mmm.
Catherine Some people might think him handsomer than his brother.
Isabella (*nodding*) No.
Catherine Though his air is more assuming, and I think his countenance less prepossessing.
Isabella (*not altogether in agreement*) Mmm.

Tilney (*arriving, suddenly*) Miss Thorpe: my brother, Captain Tilney, wonders if you might have any objection to dancing with him.
Isabella (*brightly*) Oh!
Catherine (*swiftly, confident*) No, Mr Tilney, no indeed, Miss Thorpe does not mean to dance at all this evening. She is quite decided. Of course, please thank your brother; but I fear that dancing is impossible.

A beat. Isabella smiles her agreement and, looking bashful, wanders off, her gaze drifting every so often towards Captain Tilney. In the background, the orchestra starts to play

It is very good-natured of your brother to ask. I suppose he saw Isabella without a partner and fancied she might wish for one. But he is quite mistaken, for she would not dance upon any account in the world.
Tilney How very little trouble it can give you to understand the motive of other people's actions.
Catherine Why? What do you mean?
Tilney With you, it is not "How is somebody likely to be influenced? What is the inducement most likely to act upon other people's feelings, age or situation?" but rather "How should *I* be influenced? What would be *my* inducement to act in such a way?"
Catherine I do not understand you.
Tilney But I understand you perfectly well.
Catherine Me? Well, yes. I cannot speak well enough to be unintelligible; but tell me what you mean.

During Tilney's next speech we see Isabella dance across the back of the stage with Captain Tilney

Tilney I meant only that your attributing my brother's wish of dancing with Miss Thorpe to good nature alone, convinced me of your being superior in good nature yourself to all the rest of the world.
Catherine (*seeing Isabella; in astonishment, faintly*) I cannot think how it could happen. Isabella was so determined not to dance.
Tilney And did Isabella never change her mind before?
Catherine Oh! But … because … and what of your brother?
Tilney The fairness of your friend was an open attraction. Her firmness, you know, could only be understood by yourself. (*He moves away*)

The dance concludes. Tilney encounters his brother; Catherine runs to Isabella

Isabella (*not looking Catherine in the eye*) He is such a rattle! Amusing

enough, if my mind had not been disengaged, but I would have given the world to sit still.
Catherine Then why did you not?
Isabella Oh my dear! It would have looked so particular, and you know how I abhor doing that. I refused him as long as I possibly could, but he would take no denial. You have no idea how he pressed me; and it was not merely that he wanted to dance — he wanted to dance with *me*. Oh I am so glad it is over! My spirits are quite jaded with listening to his nonsense: and then, being such a smart young fellow, I saw every eye was upon us ...

Eleanor appears

Eleanor Miss Morland? Please excuse me, but ——

Mrs Allen bursts in on them

Mrs Allen Oh my dear Isabella, Mr Morland is returned. Mrs Thorpe and I have been searching high and low for you ...
Isabella (*disconcerted*) Mr Morland? James? Oh — how wonderful. How perfect. Catherine, your brother is come back. Are you not pleased?
Catherine *I*? Pleased?
Isabella As happy as I am, for we are sisters now, our hearts shall feel alike in everything.
Mrs Allen Hurry, hurry — Mr Morland is in agony until he sees you, Isabella.
Isabella (*suddenly happy*) Of course!

And Isabella leaves with Mrs Allen

Scene 30

The Invitation

Eleanor has been waiting for her moment

Eleanor Oh my dear Miss Morland. I have sad news. My father has determined that we shall all quit Bath by the end of the week.
Catherine (*horrified*) No!
Eleanor Yes. my father can seldom be prevailed on to give the waters what I think a fair trial, but if perhaps — perhaps you would be so good, it would make me very happy if ——

The General stamps in

General Eleanor, have you been successful in your invitation to your friend?
Eleanor I was just beginning to make the request, sir ...
General Well proceed. I know how much your heart is in it .

Eleanor makes to speak, but the General carries on

My daughter, Miss Morland, has been forming a very bold wish. We leave Bath on Saturday. And could we carry our selfish point with you, we should leave it without a single regret. Can you, in short, be prevailed on to quit this scene of public triumph, and oblige your friend Eleanor with your company in Gloucestershire? If you can be induced to honour us with a visit, you will make us happy beyond expression. 'Tis true, we can offer you nothing like the gaieties of this lively place — yet no endeavours shall be wanting on our side to make your stay at Northanger Abbey not wholly disagreeable.

Music. A moment of magic and excitement

Catherine (*thrilled*) Northanger Abbey?
General Mrs Allen has already given her approval. Since she can consent to part with you, we may expect philosophy from all the world! Come, Eleanor.

They go

Catherine is beside herself with joy. She addresses the audience

Catherine Catherine was now convinced of being favoured beyond every other human creature, in friends and fortune, circumstance and chance. Her feelings, her preferences had each known the happiness of a return. Wherever she felt attachment, she had been able to create it. She was to be the chosen visitor of the Tilneys, she was to be for weeks under the same roof with the person whose society she most prized and, in addition to all the rest, this roof was to be the roof of an Abbey!

The Count de Vereza appears behind her. A few bars of the courtly Venetian theme play

Vereza Within seven days we shall be together in Udolpho!

Scene 31

Four hundred pounds a year

Catherine's enthusiasm is punctured by the arrival of Isabella, looking martyred, followed by James, looking worried, and Mrs Allen, looking concerned

Catherine James!
Isabella Your brother has explained to me the kind intentions of your father.
Catherine Oh — good!
James He will resign me a living ——
Isabella — of about four hundred pounds yearly value.
James A living of which our father is himself the incumbent ——
Mrs Allen This is generous!
James — as soon as I am old enough to take it.
Isabella (*very martyred*) In *two* or *three* years.
Mrs Allen (*brightly*) That represents no trifling deduction from his father's income.
James And he promises an estate of equal value in the future.
Isabella It is not on my account that I wish for more; but I cannot bear to be the means of injuring my dear Morland, making him suffer an income hardly enough to keep one in the common necessaries of life. For myself, it is nothing. I *hate* money. But you have found me out. The long, long, endless years that are to pass before your brother here can hold the living. That's the sting.
James Oh Isabella. Your good kind heart. I too must suffer this delay, but though it is unwelcome, I can bear it for your sake…
Isabella (*"to say the very least"*) Unwelcome…?
Mrs Allen Of course it is unwelcome. We perfectly see into your heart, and everybody must love you the better for such a noble honest affection.

And Isabella hugs Mrs Allen, and Catherine hugs James

Isabella dances off with James — a little formally, perhaps

Vereza reappears. The Venetian theme plays again

Vereza Only three days … only three days.

Scene 32

Giddy Isabella

Catherine (*to the audience*) Catherine's uncomfortable feelings begin to lessen. She endeavoured to believe that the delay of the marriage was the only source of Isabella's regret, and, when she saw her at their next meeting as cheerful and amiable as ever, endeavoured to forget that she had for a minute thought otherwise.

Isabella dashes up, laughing, merry, teasing

Isabella I have just had a letter from John. You can guess the contents.
Catherine No indeed I cannot.
Isabella You *know* he is over head and ears in love with you.
Catherine With me, dear Isabella!
Isabella Nay, my sweet Catherine, his attentions were such as a child must have noticed. You gave him the most positive encouragement. He says that he as good as made you an offer, and that you received his advances in the kindest way.
Catherine (*appalled*) As to any attentions on his side, I never had the smallest idea of it for a moment. And as to making me an offer, or anything like it, there must be some unaccountable mistake. Pray undeceive him as soon as you can.

Isabella sulks

My dear friend you must not be angry with me. I cannot suppose your brother cares so very much about me. And you know we shall still be sisters.
Isabella (*blushing*) Yes, yes, there are more ways than one of our being sisters — but where am I wandering to?

Music surges up, then underscores the rest of this scene

Isabella moves away, meets Captain Tilney and dances with him

Catherine (*to the audience*) What did she mean by that? Oh I am in despair! It seems that Captain Tilney is falling in love with Isabella and Isabella is, without realizing it, encouraging him. It must be unconscious — oh, it must, it *must* — for Isabella is in love with James. I cannot, cannot doubt her truth, her good intentions.

Isabella (*moving to Catherine*) I would not for the world hurry you into an engagement with my brother. Above all things, my dear Catherine, do not be in a hurry, you will certainly live to repent it. Frederick says there is nothing people are so often deceived in as the state of their own affections, and I believe he is very right.

Isabella and Captain Tilney dance off again

James enters and watches them dance

Catherine (*to herself*) "Frederick"? What can she mean by such unsteady conduct? She cannot be unaware of the pain she is causing. It is so thoughtless of her! So wilful! James is unhappy, anyone can see. Grave and uneasy ... I cannot bear to watch it. And poor Captain Tilney! He will be disappointed. Isabella is engaged to James. To *James!*

SCENE 33

Tilney's view

Catherine sees Tilney

Catherine Mr Tilney! I beg you to tell your brother of Miss Thorpe's engagement to James.
Tilney My brother does know it.
Catherine Does he? Then why does he stay here? The longer he stays, the worse it will be for him at last. He can have no hope here, and it is only staying to be miserable.
Tilney (*smiling*) I am sure my brother would not wish that.
Catherine Then you will persuade him to go away.
Tilney I cannot begin to persuade him.
Catherine But he does not know the pain he is giving my brother.
Tilney Is it Frederick's attentions to Miss Thorpe, or Miss Thorpe's admission of them that gives your brother pain?
Catherine (*after a moment*) Isabella is wrong, but I am sure she cannot mean to torment, for she is very much attached to my brother; she has been in love with him ever since they first met.
Tilney I understand: she is in love with James, and flirts with Frederick.
Catherine Oh no, not flirts. A woman in love with one man cannot flirt with another.
Tilney It is probable that she will neither love so well nor flirt so well as she might do either singly.

Catherine (*after a moment*) Then you do not believe Isabella so very much attached to my brother? Oh. Poor James.

Tilney Miss Morland, Miss Morland! In this amiable concern for your brother's comfort, may you not be a little mistaken? Would he thank you for supposing that her affection is only to be secured by her seeing nothing of Captain Tilney? Is he safe only in solitude? He cannot think this and you may be sure he would not have you think it. I will not say "Do not be uneasy", because I know that you are so at this moment; but be as little uneasy as you can. Their hearts are open to each other as neither heart can be to you; they know exactly what is required and what can be borne.

Catherine I do not know. It seems so dangerous. So difficult.

Music starts, and, in the background, three couples begin to dance. The sixth set piece. [See Music Plot]

Tilney Though Frederick will not leave Bath with us, he will probably remain but a very short time, perhaps only a few days behind us. His leave of absence will soon expire, and he must return to his regiment. And what will then be their acquaintance? The mess room will drink Isabella Thorpe for a fortnight, and she will laugh with your brother over poor Tilney's passion for a month. (*A beat*) Miss Morland. Will you dance? I think there is still time.

And after a moment Tilney and Catherine join the dance. And the Lights burn brightly on the dancing couples, and slowly die, leaving a single light on James which in turn fades to darkness

ACT II

Scene 1

Leaving Bath

The sound of rain. Servants with umbrellas manoeuvre bags onto a carriage. Horses stamp and snort

The General — brusque, brisk, impatient — is in the midst of it all, with Catherine. There is a low murmur from the others

General (*shouting*) Two boxes behind, one under the *front* seat, the grey trunk on *top*! It is now past ten o'clock, Sam! We are five minutes behind our time; NOT GOOD, NOT GOOD! Where's my *coat*? No, Peter! Put it in the carriage, Peter! Wool-gathering, Peter! What's that thing? No room for it — get rid of it.
Catherine General, it is my writing desk.
General Ah, well, put it on the back bench — well then *make* room for it, sir! Where is the middle seat? Well, sir, it can be drawn out *now*! My dear Miss Morland, it is abominably crowded in here ... my daughter's wretched parcels ... why do you not travel in the curricle with my son?

At this, the servants undo what they have done, and begin to move the baggage off, to the other carriage

I am anxious you should see as much of the country as possible — BRIDGET! Tidy the seat — not higgledy piggledy, woman, *stack* them, just *so*! SAM! It is now TEN MINUTES AFTER TEN O'CLOCK; confound you, sir, the leading harness is a full stop loose!

Scene 2

The Journey

There is the sound of trotting hooves. Tilney and Catherine sit side by side

Tilney I am grateful to you, Miss Morland, for agreeing to be my sister's guest at Northanger.

Catherine (*so happy; gazing out*) He drove so well, so *quietly*, without any disturbance, without parading to Catherine, or swearing at the horses ——
Tilney My sister's circumstances are to some degree uncomfortable ——
Catherine —— and then his hat sat so well, and the innumerable capes of his great coat looked so —— important...
Tilney She has no female companion, and, when my father is away, can find herself without any companion at all.
Catherine (*turning to Tilney*) But are you not with her?
Tilney Northanger is only half my home. My own house is at Woodston, twenty miles distant from my father's. Some of my time is necessarily spent there.
Catherine How sorry you must be for that! After being used to such a home as the Abbey, an ordinary parsonage house must be very disagreeable.
Tilney You have formed a very favourable idea of the abbey.
Catherine Is it not a fine old place, just like what one reads about?
Tilney And are you prepared to encounter all the horrors that a building such as "what one reads about" may produce? Have you a stout heart? Nerves fit for sliding panels and tapestry?
Catherine Oh yes, I should not easily be frightened, because there would be so many people in the house; and besides, it has never been uninhabited and left deserted for years and then the family come back to it unawares, without giving any notice, as generally happens.
Tilney No, certainly.

SCENE 3

Gothic possibilities

A beat. The Lights dim slightly, the wind gets up. We become aware of a door, set back in the shadows; an important door for this second act

Tilney (*utterly straight-faced*) But you must be aware that when a young lady is introduced into a dwelling of this kind, she is always lodged apart from the rest of the family.
Catherine (*taken in*) Indeed?
Tilney While they snugly repair to their own end of the house, she is put in the charge of Annette, the ancient housekeeper.

Annette pops up: shrinking, fearful, superstitious. Catherine sees her, and hears her dark French accent. Tilney doesn't

She will take you along many gloomy passages ——
Annette Into an apartment never used since some cousin died in it, oh, twenty years ago.

Tilney Will not your mind misgive you, when you find yourself in the gloomy chamber, with only the feeble rays of a dying fire to take in its size?
Catherine (*nervous/thrilled*) Oh! But this will not happen to me, I am sure.
Tilney You will examine the furniture of your apartment; a broken lute, perhaps, a ponderous chest which no efforts can open. Annette gazes on you in great agitation, and drops a few unintelligible hints ...
Annette It has been closed since... I dare not tell you why ... You must not open it unless...
Tilney To raise your spirits she tells you:
Annette This part of the abbey is haunted!
Catherine Haunted!
Annette And no servants within call ...
Tilney And no lock upon the door!
Catherine Oh Mr Tilney, how dreadful! But I am sure this cannot really happen to me. I am sure your housekeeper is not called Annette!
Annette (*retreating; in disgust*) Pah!
Catherine Well, what then?
Tilney On the third night you will probably have a violent storm, and during the frightful gusts of wind that accompany it, you will discern one part of a tapestry more violently agitated than the rest. Behind this you discover a large old-fashioned chest of ebony and gold. You eagerly advance to it, unlock its folding doors, and search in every drawer. You discover nothing of importance, except perhaps for a considerable hoard of diamonds, but at last a secret spring is touched, an inner compartment opens, a roll of paper appears. You seize it and read!

A voice speaks; the words seem to echo down long corridors

Voice Oh thou, whomsoever thou mayst be, into whose hands these memoirs of the wretched Matilda may fall...
Tilney But suddenly, your lamp expires, and leaves you in total darkness!
Catherine Oh! No, no, do not say so. Well, go on!
Tilney (*laughing*) No, Miss Morland, you must make up the rest. Besides, we have arrived.

SCENE 4

Northanger Abbey

Servants sweep on and help Catherine and Tilney down from the carriage. Music plays, elegant and civilized

Servant 1 To find herself with such ease in the very precincts of the abbey ——

Servant 2 — and driven along a smooth, level road without obstacle, alarm or solemnity of any kind —
Catherine — struck her as odd and inconsistent.
Servant 1 The breeze had not seemed to waft the sighs of the murdered to her.
Servant 2 It had wafted nothing but the scent of freshly cut grass.

The General and Eleanor step forward

General Welcome to Northanger Abbey, Miss Morland!
Catherine Thank you, thank you!
Eleanor Inside, the furniture was in all the profusion of elegance and modern taste.
Catherine (*horrified*) And the windows ——
General We have preserved them in their gothic form with all due care.
Catherine — were so large, so clear, so light! To an imagination which had hoped for the smallest panes and the heaviest stone-work, for painted glass, dirt and cobwebs, the difference was *very* distressing.
General I fear you will find our life here dull, Miss Morland. It is a dead time of year. No wild fowl, no game, and the Lady Frasers not in the country. Mmmm. We can at least show you the house! Henry departs for his parish in the morning. When he has gone, we shall make a tour: the house, and then the shrubberies and garden. Let us hope the weather will improve. Dinner to be on table directly!

Scene 5

James and Isabella

The focus shifts, suddenly, back to Bath

James Jealous! Do I not have some reason to be jealous!
Isabella It is intolerable. My spirit is independent, Mr Morland; I will come and go as I please — yes! — and dance with Captain Tilney if I choose to. Indeed, I am sorry, dreadfully sorry, to find you so demanding and unreasonable.
James You have not spoken to me this evening, except for this reproach. Last night we sat together, but your eyes were always bent to the one door or the other, watching and waiting for the Captain of Dragoons!
Isabella Am I not now to look away from you! Fie, you would have me locked up in a room! You would play the sultan, and keep me only for yourself!
James Yes! I would.

Act II, Scene 6   53

Isabella What! Always to be watched, in person or by proxy! If there is one emotion I detest, it is jealousy.

Isabella breaks away from James and leaves

James (*to himself*) And you have often said that the one virtue you admire is constancy!

Scene 6

Frightening furniture

We switch from this argument to Catherine's bedroom

Firelight, dancing shadows. Rain, wind against the shutters. Windows rattling. There are shadowy figures just beyond the light. They wear masks and cloaks

Catherine As Catherine entered her room, she listened to the wind and rain with awe …

A door bangs. Catherine starts

(*Whistling in the dark*) How glad I am that Northanger is what it is! If it had been like some other places, I do not know that, in such a night as this, I could have answered for my courage …

Creepy music

Tilney's Voice (*a chill tone now; echoing*) Will not your mind misgive you, when you find yourself in this gloomy chamber, with only the feeble rays of the fire to take in its size …
Catherine (*nervously*) But now to be sure, there is nothing to alarm one.
Tilney's Voice You will examine the furniture of your apartment ——
Catherine Yes, yes! Handsome, comfortable — walls papered — not a stitch of tapestry …
Tilney's Voice A ponderous chest?

A curtain twitches aside. A chest is revealed

Catherine This is strange indeed! I did not expect such a sight as this! An immense, heavy chest! What can it hold? Why should it be placed there? Pushed back, as if it meant to be out of sight! I will look into it; cost me what it may, I will look into it …

Tilney's Voice A lock of silver, tarnished with age, the lid mysteriously heavy ...

Catherine looks around nervously. Suspense builds. A clock ticks. Eerie music trickles round her. She pushes and pushes at the lid of the chest; it eventually opens. She gasps, looks in, then reaches into it and pulls out — six pillows. Just then there is a knock at the door. The music stops abruptly. Catherine struggles to hide the pillows

Eleanor enters

Eleanor (*brightly*) That is a curious old chest, is it not? It is impossible to say how many generations it has been here. Useful for bed-linen. But it is so difficult to open. In that corner it is at least out of the way.
Catherine (*deeply embarrassed*) I was looking for — looking for ——
Eleanor (*helpfully*) Pillows. Of course. I like a good quantity of pillows myself. (*She stacks an impossibly high mound of pillows on the bed*) And are you comfortable, Miss Morland? Is everything to your liking?
Catherine Oh yes.
Eleanor Well then, good-night, dear Miss Morland. I am so glad that you are here with us.
Catherine And I am more than glad to be your guest. How kind of you, dear Miss Tilney.
Eleanor Good-night.
Catherine Good-night.

The door shuts on Catherine. Creepy music starts again

Good-night... (*A beat*) I shall take my time. I shall not, under any circumstances, *hurry*. I am completely at ease. The noise is the noise of the wind. These curtains hide nothing but the window. (*But she checks the curtains nonetheless*) The bed hides no secret stairwell. (*But she checks this, too*) The chest *was* only full of pillows. (*She decides not to check this again*) Who would be afraid? Who could be other than complacent? What could possibly disturb a person's calm?

The Lights shift and a large cabinet is revealed in the corner of the room

What is that cabinet? I had not noticed it before.
Tilney's Voice (*gothic again*) A large, old-fashioned cabinet of ebony and gold ...
Catherine Not *exactly* gold. Black and yellow. *Like* gold. (*Faintly*) Oh. (*A beat*) I shall go to sleep. A black and yellow cabinet. How tedious. How commonplace. (*And she snuggles down into the bed*)

Act II, Scene 7

Tilney's Voice Impelled by an irresistible presentiment, you unlock its folding doors and search in every drawer.

Catherine sits up again and stares at the cabinet

At last a secret spring is touched, an inner compartment opens; a roll of paper appears ——
Catherine (*faintly*) What a remarkable coincidence. Just as Mr Tilney said. (*She takes a deep breath*) It can do no harm to look ... (*She gets out of bed and advances on the cabinet. With extravagant casualness, she opens the door. It squeaks*) Ah. Drawers. I shall look at just one or two. (*She looks in every one*) Well there! I never had the smallest idea of finding anything in any part of it. Ha! Who would ever be so foolish as to imagine that bedroom cabinets contain secret springs and inner compartments? Ha! (*She bangs on a panel to prove her point. And then another. And again, more confidently*)

Suddenly, another panel springs open with a loud crack

(*Yelping*) Ah! (*She reaches into the inner compartment, and, trembling, searches the interior. The tension builds. She pulls out — a scroll of papers!*) OH! Oh, oh, OHH!! (*She stumbles over, collects her lamp, staggers to the middle of the room and sets the lamp on the floor. She tries to unravel the scroll*) Oh no! Oh no oh no oh no!

The Light flickers, fades and goes out

Catherine whimpers with fear and buries herself in a heap of bedding in the middle of the floor

The storm rises. In the darkness we hear banging and moaning, the wind howling, doors rattling

Scene 7

The Big Booby

The Lights come up brightly. It is the next morning

Eleanor enters to find Catherine still buried in the heap of bedding

Eleanor Miss Morland? Catherine?
Catherine (*waking suddenly*) The scroll! The scroll! How is it to be explained? What can be written there? What can it contain?

Eleanor (*passing over this; brightly*) Did you pass a pleasant night?
Catherine I discovered it — in the cabinet. How long has it been there?
Eleanor (*faintly alarmed*) How long has what been where?
Catherine The scroll! The ancient scroll!
Eleanor (*more alarmed*) The ancient scroll?
Catherine Here it is! Read it. Read it!
Eleanor (*frightened*) Who knows what it might say?
Catherine (*dramatically*) You alone will know!
Eleanor (*uncertainly*) Yes, yes of course... (*A beat; then, reading carefully*) "To wash and press: two shirts, six pairs of stockings, three cravats, a frilled stock, one evening waistcote." (*A beat; next sheet*) "Three shirts, four pairs of stockings, one cravat, *two* waistcotes." (*A beat; next sheet*) "To poultice chestnut mare for bruising to right leading flank: five shillings and sixpence..."

A beat. Catherine is now very small indeed

Catherine (*in a very, very small voice*) I thought they might be ——
Eleanor Foolish Matilda!
Catherine (*starting*) Mat?
Eleanor The careless girl never clears out these bedrooms thoroughly. I shall certainly speak to her. How kind of you to bring the matter to my attention.

There is the sound of a gong, beaten impatiently in the hall below

(*A little on edge*) But come, Miss Morland. My father has changed his mind. He will show us the gardens first, although it is so early — and make use, he says, of the present "smiling weather". The Abbey we may see later. He is waiting for us downstairs. Do not be uneasy; he always walks out at this time of day.

And Eleanor exits

Mortified, Catherine picks up the bedding, throws it down and stamps on it. Then she grabs her jacket and hat and moves to leave

Annette appears in the shadows

Creepy music plays

Annette (*spookily*) Strange...
Catherine (*as though reminded of a secret thought*) Strange?
Annette She seemed to be ——

Act II, Scene 8

Catherine — embarrassed.
Annette The General will show you the Abbey "later"...
Catherine I would like to see it now!
Annette But he says "later"...
Catherine Can he be unwilling to show me the Abbey?
Annette And it is strangely early ——
Catherine Why did Eleanor believe that I might be uneasy?
Annette And it is odd ——
Catherine (*ahead of her*) — that he should *always* take his walk so early ...

Scene 8

The Kitchen Garden

A burst of merry music. A sudden switch. The bed is removed

The General and Eleanor arrive

The Lights brighten to a March exterior

General The kitchen garden covers five acres. Fourteen hothouses over *there;* ten gardeners, a dozen boys, assorted women. My gardeners *matter* to me, Miss Morland. What do you think? What do you think, Miss Morland?
Catherine I have never in my life seen gardens to equal them. So large, so many different beds and borders!
General (*with vanity*) Larger then Allen's? Really? Well, though I have not the least ambition to outshine even my neighbour, I do believe these gardens are unrivalled in the kingdom.
Catherine Mr Allen does not care about the garden — never goes into it.
General Indeed? He is a happy man! But how are Mr Allen's forcing houses worked? My central hothouse has four others built alongside, with a quantity of ducts and vents to control the passage of hot air ...
Catherine Mr Allen has only one hothouse for Mrs Allen's plants. When they are cold.

A beat

Eleanor Let us walk back through Fir Tree Wood.
Catherine (*immediately excited*) Oh yes!
General No, no, it is cold and unhealthy, and besides, the sun is shining!
Catherine Oh. But it looks so beautiful — dark and mysterious.
General If *you* say so, Miss Morland. Forgive me, though; the rays of the

sun are not too cheerful for me. I shall meet you in the Lower Drawing
Room. Ten minutes, Eleanor!

SCENE 9

Mrs Tilney

The General leaves

The Light changes. A dark, woody, green place. The girls link arms

Catherine Oh — wonderful!
Eleanor I am particularly fond of this spot. It was my mother's favourite walk.

Immediately, figures stir in the shadows

I used to walk here so often with her! Though I never loved it then as I have loved it since. Her memory endears it now.
Catherine (*bravely*) And ought it not to endear it to her husband? Yet the General would not enter it.

Eleanor sighs

Catherine Her death must have been a great affliction.
Eleanor (*low*) A great and increasing one. I was only thirteen when it happened, and did not, could not, then know what a loss it was. I have no sister and, though Henry is a great deal here, it is impossible for me not to be often solitary.
Catherine You must miss him very much.
Eleanor A mother would have been always present. A mother would have been a constant friend; her influence would have been beyond all other.
Catherine Tell me about her, please. Was she a very charming woman?
Eleanor Oh yes, oh yes.
Catherine And was she handsome?
Eleanor Yes *indeed*.
Catherine Is there a picture of her in the Abbey?
Eleanor Yes, there is...
Catherine (*with a design behind the question*) Why did she like this place? (*A beat*) The melancholy shade is so agreeable. Was she ... dejected often?
Annette (*softly, from the shadows*) Often ...
Catherine (*craftily*) Her picture, I suppose, hangs in your father's room?
Eleanor No. It was intended for the drawing room, but my father was dissatisfied with the painting, and hid it away. After her death, I found it,

Act II, Scene 10

and hung it in my bed-chamber. Where I shall be happy to show it to you. It is very like. (*A beat*) Forgive me Catherine. I must run ahead to find my father. Please excuse me.

And Eleanor runs off, hiding tears. Music plays

Annette (*coming forward*) Dejected often...
Catherine An unkind husband.
Annette He did not love her walk.
Catherine Could he have loved *her*?
Annette A handsome man ——
Catherine — but cruelty in his face!
Annette Cruel to women?
Catherine Cruel to his wife!
Annette And the portrait ——
Catherine (*shocked*) — hid away!
Annette Too good a likeness...
Catherine Not valued by the *husband*. Oh, what a cruel, cruel man. Odious. He is my absolute aversion. To be so cruel to such a *charming* woman...
Annette Oh, ma'm'selle Emily!
Catherine (*momentarily confused*) Emily?

Scene 10

The Tour

The Lights change

General (*off*) This way. Come along, Eleanor.

Eleanor and the General rejoin Catherine

The picture's by a man called Opie. *Boy with Swine*. Persuasive, don't you think?

Each part of the house they visit is represented by a different light falling on them, along with appropriate sound effects. The group keeps still, just turning in different directions for each new location. They start by turning to face us

Principal Drawing Room! Furniture by Mr Holland. The vases over there are Worcester; do you like the birds, my dear Miss Morland? Birds of paradise, *exotic* birds; but not by any means the prettiest creature in the room! *The Library!*

The Lights switch. A clock ticks. They face to the left

Baumgarten did these shelves here: beautiful work — morocco, full morocco. Over here: antiquities, Latin and Greek — and this is *history*, Miss Morland. Now we shall all know where to find you of a morning! Ha! These shelves move back and forth — my own idea. I think it neat. *The Cloister*!

The Lights switch. Echoey acoustic. The sound of an iron gate swinging open

— or what remains of it. My father had the greater part removed.
Catherine No!
General Decayed and derelict. I cannot think why he retained this corner.
Catherine I am relieved he did. What are these doors?
General Locked and sealed, Miss Morland. In ancient days they opened on a range of cells. The Romish monks lived here. Let us pass on ——

The Lights change again. They are by a door

Eleanor, why have you brought us here? Where are you going? What more is there to see? Miss Morland must be tired, and has surely seen all that could be worth her notice. Come, let us go back. Your friend might be glad of some refreshment after so much exercise.

The General marches away

Scene 11

Murder?

Eleanor and Catherine move away from the door, though Catherine hangs back, reluctant to leave

Catherine What door was that?
Eleanor It was my mother's room. The room in which she died.

Eleanor makes to go. Catherine stops her. Gothic figures materialize in the background.

Catherine It remains as it was, I suppose?
Eleanor Yes — entirely.
Catherine And how long ago may it be that your mother died?
Eleanor She has been dead these nine years.

Act II, Scene 12   61

Catherine You were with her to the last, I suppose.
Eleanor No. I was unfortunately from home. Her illness was sudden and short. Before I arrived, it was all over.

And Eleanor slips away, fearful of a new display of emotion. Annette creeps forward

Catherine Could it be possible? Could Henry's father … ?
Annette Oh ma'm'selle, ma'am'selle!
Catherine She was away from home!
Annette Sent away, perhaps!
Catherine Her mother was a healthy woman!
Annette (*moaning*) We cannot stay in this place!
Catherine A sudden illness? It was poison! Which did he use, I wonder?
Annette The hothouses! The hothouses!
Catherine But of course, he can breed any plant he likes: dry them, distill them, mix them at his leisure ——

A gong sounds

Annette (*alarmed*) Dinner!
Catherine — and apply them to his victim's food!
Annette You must go down to dinner…
Catherine (*after a moment, to the audience*) That evening ——
Annette Oh ma'am'selle, ma'am'selle ——
Catherine — Catherine hardly touched her food.
Annette — why would you eat so *much*!
Catherine And felt rather hungry as she sat in the drawing room afterwards with her friend.

Scene 12

Montoni?

Catherine sits and is joined by Eleanor. The General paces up and down behind them, lit spookily. The girls both read novels

Eleanor (*whispering*) My father often walks about the room in this way. It is nothing unusual.
Annette (*whispering in Catherine's ear*) It is Montoni. To the life. His air, his manner. Look at his face.

Eleanor does not hear Catherine's next line

Catherine (*to Annette*) His eyes cast down, his brow contracted. His conscience stings him!
Annette Oh unhappy man!
General (*suddenly*) Miss Morland!
Catherine Yes?
General You must be tired.

Eleanor stands, recognizing the sign to leave

Please do not feel the need to keep me company. I have many pamphlets and papers to finish before I close my eyes, and perhaps may be poring over the affairs of the nation for hours after you are asleep. Can either of us be better employed? My eyes will be blinding for the good of others and yours preparing by rest for future mischief!

Catherine curtsies to the General

The General turns and exits

Catherine My dear Miss Tilney. Eleanor.
Eleanor (*warmly*) Catherine, good-night. I take the *greatest* pleasure in your company! If I have seemed at all low-spirited, it can be only that your presence here reminds me of another's. You will forgive me?
Catherine Of course, dear Eleanor.
Eleanor Good-night.
Catherine Good-night.

Scene 13

Proof Positive

Darkness

Catherine is alone

Annette comes forward, with a candle

Annette He is still awake!
Catherine (*disbelievingly*) Reading his pamphlets!
Annette Ha!
Catherine To be kept up for hours after all the family are in bed by stupid pamphlets is *not* very likely.
Annette (*ominously*) Unless there is some deeper reason …

Act II, Scene 13

Catherine Something which can only be done while the house sleeps ...
Annette (*after a moment; gasping*) Mrs Tilney!!
Catherine Mrs Tilney! SHE LIVES! Locked away! In one of the ancient cells of the Abbey! Her gaoler — her husband. Every night he visits her, taking a plate of coarse, unwholesome food ...
Annette Praise God, she is not dead!
Catherine That's true.
Annette But we are helpless to assist her!
Catherine Her room lies just above the ancient cells which General Tilney told us were abandoned!
Annette That part of the house lies opposite your window.
Catherine I must watch.

They hurry to the front of the stage and peer out into the gloom. A beat

Catherine Nothing.
Annette No lamp.
Catherine Too early.
Annette He will go later.

A bell tolls midnight during the following

After midnight!
Catherine I shall watch till dawn!

During the following, Catherine gradually falls fast asleep on Annette's shoulder

Annette He is so calm, so fearless, so bold. He is hardened in his guilt. I remember many who have persevered in vice, moving from crime to crime, murdering and killing, without humanity or remorse, until a violent death or religious retirement closed their black careers ... Madam? (*She notices that Catherine is asleep and tuts*)

There are a few beats, then a loud cock-crow

The Lights come up; it is a bright, sunny day

Catherine (*sitting bolt upright*) I know what I must do. I shall visit the forbidden room. Alone. Poor Eleanor shall know nothing of this. It would be impossible, painful to explain. I shall search for proofs — a journal or a letter. There must be something. A secret door through which her mother was abducted! I shall go directly.
Annette (*unnecessarily*) I shall go with you!

SCENE 14

Shame!

"Edge of the seat" music

Catherine and Annette set off, and arrive at last US of the forbidden door. Mrs Tilney's room occupies the DS area

Tilney is sitting in the room, hidden from the door by the back of a wing chair

Catherine creeps into the room, tiptoes forward past the chair and throws back imaginary curtains. Light floods in. Catherine takes a deep breath, turns, sees Tilney, and screams

Annette vanishes

Tilney (*when Catherine has finished screaming*) Good-morning.
Catherine Good God! How came you here?
Tilney (*baffled*) I forget. Was it the window or the door? How came *you* here?
Catherine I came — I came to see your mother's room.
Tilney Is there anything extraordinary to be seen here?
Catherine No. No. (*She looks round and notices that Annette has gone*) Nothing at all. I thought you would return tomorrow.
Tilney I had the pleasure of finding nothing to detain me in Woodston. (*A beat*) Does Eleanor leave you to see all the rooms in the house by yourself?
Catherine Oh no. She showed me over the greater part yesterday, and we were coming here — only ... (*hushed*) your father was with us.
Tilney (*puzzled*) And that prevented you?

There is no answer

And do you like my mother's room?
Catherine (*staring round*) It is not as I expected...
Tilney It is commodious, is it not? Large and cheerful, comfortable and modern. I often sit and read in here. Eleanor sent you to look at it I suppose.
Catherine (*pale*) No.
Tilney It has been your own doing? (*A beat*) As there is nothing in the room itself to raise curiosity, this must have proceeded from respect for my mother's character, as described by Eleanor. The world, I believe, never saw a better woman. My sister, I suppose, has talked of her a great deal.
Catherine Yes, a great deal ... (*She risks the truth*) That is — no, not much.

Act II, Scene 15   65

But what she did say was very interesting. Her dying so suddenly, and you ... none of you being at home, and your father I thought, perhaps, had not been very fond of her.

Tilney (*suddenly alert*) And from these circumstances you infer, perhaps, the probability of some negligence or it may be — of something still less pardonable. (*A beat*) My mother's illness, the seizure which ended in her death *was* sudden. The malady itself was one from which she had often suffered. Three physicians attended her last days. During her illness, Frederick and I — we were both at home — saw her repeatedly, and know that she received every possible attention which could spring from the affection of those about her ——

Catherine (*hopelessly*) But your father: was *he* afflicted?

Tilney For a time greatly so. You have erred in supposing him not attached to her. He loved her, though I will not pretend that while she lived, she might not often have had much to bear. But though his temper injured her, his judgement never did. His value of her was sincere, and, if not permanently, he was truly afflicted by her death.

Catherine (*small*) I am very glad of it. It would have been very shocking...

Tilney (*forcefully*) If I understand you rightly, you had formed a surmise of such horror as I have hardly words to ... Dear Miss Morland, consider the dreadful nature of the suspicions you have entertained. What have you been judging from? Remember the country and the age in which we live. Consult your own understanding, your own sense of the probable. Does our education prepare us for such atrocities? Do our laws connive at them? Could they be perpetrated without being known, in a country like this, where every man is surrounded by a neighbourhood of voluntary spies, and where roads and newspapers lay everything open? Dearest Miss Morland — what ideas have you been admitting?

Catherine runs away from Tilney in tears

SCENE 15

No More Udolphos

Catherine runs, sobbing, out of the door and round the stage, until she reaches her own room. There she collapses

Suddenly, Annette and two Gothic characters burst in on Catherine. Creepy music plays

1st Gothic Follow me! As you value your life, we have not an instant to lose!

2nd Gothic The gates are open! We must fly! Fly!
1st Gothic They will be shut, I fear, before we can reach them.
Annette We shall soon be beyond the walls; support yourself a little longer, ma'm'selle, and all will be well.
Catherine (*recovering a little*) No.
Annette But ma'm'selle...
Catherine No!
1st Gothic What do you mean m'lady?
2nd Gothic Why this delay?
Catherine No!

There is a sudden change of light. The Gothics look around them, like vampires caught in the sun. The music stops abruptly

(*After a moment*) Mrs Radcliffe's books are very charming. I have greatly enjoyed reading them, and I know that everything she says about the Alps and the Pyrenees is perfectly correct — pine forests and vice and horrors of every description. But things are very different in Gloucestershire.
Annette Gloucestershire...?
Catherine Yes. Italy, Switzerland and the South of France may well be just as they are in *Udolpho*, and even some parts of Scotland and Cornwall, but here, in the main part of England, there is, as Henry says, some security for a woman like his mother, even if she is not loved; security in laws and manners. Murder is not tolerated.

The Gothics protest in "Oh, come off it" tones

I am *sorry*, but there it is. Servants are *not* slaves and poison cannot be procured, like rhubarb, from every druggist. It could *not* be done.
Annette (*faintly*) But the General ——
Catherine (*decidedly*) Not entirely amiable, I agree, but that does not mean he is a brute! People in the Alps and Pyrenees are clearly either good or bad, but among the English I do believe there is a general, though perhaps unequal, mixture of both. The General may not be an angel, but he is *not* a fiend. No. Not a fiend.

An awkward moment. The three Gothic characters look at one another and shrug. They start to go, still encouraging Catherine to join them

1st Gothic A French vessel sails at midnight from Marseilles...
2nd Gothic On a full gallop, we may reach Leghorn by the evening!
Annette Pray God we meet with no straggling parties of *banditti*!
1st Gothic I have a good trombone which will be of some service ...

Act II, Scene 16   67

Annette (*taking a last chance*) Let us rejoice in our escape from Udolpho, not torment ourselves with looking out for dangers that may never arrive.

But Catherine will not even look up

The Gothic characters vanish, grumbling

Catherine takes up Udolpho *and throws it away*

Scene 16

Letters From Bath

Formal, stately music

Henry and Eleanor join Catherine, and lift her up. The three dance together. This is almost a ballet. [See Music Plot] The Tilneys bring her back to the world. Catherine regains her composure

Catherine Henry's astonishing generosity and nobleness of conduct, in never alluding in the slightest way to what had happened, was of the greatest assistance to Catherine; and sooner than she had thought possible, her spirits became absolutely comfortable. Her thoughts turned to Bath. She had received no word from either Isabella or James ——
Eleanor But on the tenth day after her arrival at the Abbey ——
Tilney — Henry brought her a letter.
Catherine (*to Tilney*) 'Tis from James.

James appears "in another place", very distressed. His focus is on Catherine; her focus is the letter. Eleanor and Henry are attentive to Catherine

James Dear Catherine, it is my duty to tell you that everything is at an end between Miss Thorpe and me. I left her and Bath yesterday, never to see either again ...
Catherine Oh James, James!
James I shall not enter into particulars; they would only pain you more.

Isabella appears suddenly. She addresses James

Isabella I am going to Bristol with Captain Tilney ...
Tilney (*to Catherine*) With my brother?
Eleanor With Frederick!

James You shall soon hear enough from another quarter to know where lies the blame!
Isabella He thinks we may visit his brother and your sister at Northanger.
James I am guilty only of too easily thinking my affection returned!
Isabella There is nothing people are so often deceived in as the state of their own affections.
James Thank God. I am undeceived in time! But it is a heavy blow.
Isabella You men are so amazingly jealous. I am glad to be rid of you.
James After my father's consent had been so kindly given!
Isabella Of course your father has a right to do exactly as he likes with his money ...
James She has made me miserable forever.
Isabella Very well, let us part. Your jealousy will not be satisfied until you see me married to Captain Tilney. So be it. But it is your doubts and uncertainty that have brought this about.
James She has made me miserable for ever.
Isabella (*curtly*) Goodbye.

And she goes

Catherine (*shouting after Isabella*) You have deserted my brother! (*To herself*) I did not believe there was such inconstancy and fickleness and everything that is bad in the world!
Tilney (*to Catherine*) Frederick marrying Miss Thorpe is not probable. Your brother must be mistaken.
James (*still reciting the letter to Catherine*) I wish your visit to Northanger may be over before Captain Tilney makes his engagement known.
Tilney Well, if it is so, then all is over with Frederick. He is a deceased man, defunct in understanding.
James I cannot understand what she would be at, for there could be no need of my being played off to make her secure of Tilney!
Tilney (*ironically*) Prepare for your sister-in-law, Eleanor: open, candid, artless, guileless, with affections strong but simple ...
Catherine She may behave well by *your* family. Now she has really got the man she likes, she may be constant.
Tilney Unless a baronet should come her way; that is Frederick's only chance.
James (*turning to go*) Dearest Catherine, beware how you give your heart ...
Catherine I was never so deceived in anyone's character in my life before.

Isabella returns with another letter. Time has passed. She is not so cocky now. She reads from a letter she has written to Catherine. Catherine ignores her; Isabella tries to gain her attention

Isabella My *dearest* Catherine ——
Tilney (*to Catherine*) You feel, I suppose, that in losing Isabella, you lose half yourself.
Isabella You are dearer to me than anybody can conceive.
Tilney You feel a void in your heart which nothing else will occupy.
Isabella I am quite uneasy about your dear brother, and am fearful of some misunderstanding. He is the only man I ever did or could love, and I trust you will convince him of it. The spring fashions are partly down, and the hats the most frightful you can imagine ...
Tilney You feel that you have no longer any friend to whom you can speak without reserve.
Isabella (*nervously*) Captain Tilney was amazingly disposed to follow and tease me after you went away. He became quite my shadow.
Tilney You feel you have no friend on whose counsel you could rely. You feel all this.
Catherine (*after a moment's reflection*) No. I do not — ought I?
Isabella Many girls would have been taken in, but I know the fickle sex too well. He went away two days ago ... (*she is lost for a moment*) ... he is the greatest coxcomb I ever saw, and amazingly disagreeable. The last two days he was always by the side of Charlotte Davies ...
Catherine To say the truth, though I am hurt and grieved that I cannot still love her, that I am never to see her again, I do not feel so very, very much afflicted as one would have thought.
Isabella (*approaching Catherine*) I wear nothing but purple now: it is your dear brother's favourite colour. I know I look hideous in it, but no matter. Lose no time, my dearest, sweetest Catherine, in writing to him and to me ...

Isabella puts the letter directly into Catherine's hand, and goes

Scene 17

Farewell Isabella

Catherine So much for Isabella! And for all our intimacy! She must think me an idiot or she would not have written so. I see what she has been about. She is a vain coquette, and her tricks have not answered. I do not believe she had ever any regard either for James or for me. And I wish I had never known her.
Eleanor It will soon be as if you never had.
Catherine And your brother...?
Tilney He has his vanities as well as Miss Tilney.

Catherine You do not think he ever really cared for her?
Tilney I am persuaded that he never did.
Catherine There is no great harm done, because I do not think Isabella has any heart to lose. But suppose he had made her very much in love with him.
Tilney We must first suppose Isabella to have had a heart to lose …
Catherine (*after a moment*) I have imposed on your generosity too long. I must return to Fullerton.
Eleanor But I had hoped for the pleasure of your company for a much longer time. If Mr and Mrs Morland were aware of how agreeable it is for me to have you here, they would be too generous to hasten your return.
Catherine Oh — Papa and Mama are in no hurry at all. For my own pleasure I could stay with you as long again.
Eleanor (*grasping her hand*) Then say "so be it".
Catherine So be it.
Tilney You could not have made us more happy. We rejoice in your company, and shall always remember that this time was made special by it. Thank you. Thank you indeed.

Music begins. The idyll

Eleanor Our father has a project for this Wednesday. We are to visit Henry's parsonage at Woodston.
Tilney (*imitating his father*) Monday will be a busy day with you, we will not come on Monday, and Tuesday ——

The General joins them, carrying Catherine's coat

General (*taking over from his son*) — and Tuesday will be a busy one with me. I cannot in decency fail attending the club. But on Wednesday, Henry, you may expect us!
Catherine (*comforted*) Is it a pretty place?

The General walks to Catherine with her coat

General See for yourself, Miss Morland.

Scene 18

The Woodston Idyll

Music and dappled light

We see the corner of a fine stone house, a pastoral scene stretching away beyond. A servant girl comes forward and presents Catherine with a great basket of flowers. Catherine gasps at the beauty of it all

Catherine (*reciting a letter*) Dear Mrs Allen, Woodston has so many recommendations. The house stands among fine meadows facing the south-east, with an excellent kitchen garden. The Abbey is now no more to me than any other house, but how perfect is the unpretending comfort of a parsonage. My heart was very full when we arrived. I prefer it to any place I have ever been at. The house is beautifully furnished — except for the drawing room... (*To Tilney*) Oh, why do you not fit up this room, Mr Tilney? What a pity not to have it fitted up! It is the prettiest room I ever saw: it is the prettiest room in the world!
General I trust that it will very speedily be furnished: it waits only for a lady's taste.
Catherine (*to the General*) If it was my house, I should never sit anywhere else. And look at the cottage there among the trees. Oh, it is the prettiest cottage.
General You like it, you approve it; it is enough. Henry! Remember that Robinson is spoken to. The cottage remains!

During the following speech, the scene shifts back to Catherine's fire-warmed, candlelit bedroom in the Abbey. Once it is set, Catherine curls up on her bed, and continues to write her letter. The music continues

Catherine (*the letter again*) Never has a day passed so quickly! We walked through the ornamental garden and the meadows to the village, then back for dinner at four. By six we were in the General's carriage and driving back to the Abbey. Henry is so kind to me. I wish I understood his true wishes — the true feelings of his heart ... Shortly after our trip to Woodston, the General departed for London. We now await his return. I can hardly describe the happiness of the last few days. We do as we wish, laugh when we want to, enjoy every meal, come and go as we please. Henry has now returned to Woodston for two days. This lessens our gaiety but not our comfort ...

SCENE 19

Exile

Suddenly: the crash of a huge door slamming shut. The music stops, abruptly. Silence

Catherine looks up, startled. After a moment, the sound of a cry; Eleanor's voice, obviously deeply distressed

Eleanor (*off*) No! I can not!

Catherine is alarmed

Eleanor appears at the door, distraught and sobbing.

Catherine Eleanor!
Eleanor My dear Catherine, you must not, you must not indeed ... I cannot bear it — I come to you on such an errand ...
Catherine Errand! To me?
Eleanor How shall I tell you? Oh, how shall I tell you? It is my father ——
Catherine Yes?

The General himself strides in, pale and angry

General (*to Eleanor*) Have you told her yet?
Eleanor I cannot do it.
General You have forgotten. Let me remind you, Eleanor. We leave for Hereford on Monday. Your friend departs for Fullerton tomorrow ——
Eleanor Father!
General At seven.
Eleanor Send a servant with her. I beg you! It is the very least ——
General She is not used to servants. She shall find her own way home.
Eleanor But a journey of seventy miles ——
General Her artfulness will see her back to Fullerton ...
Eleanor What reason can there be for this — this cruelty?
General She knows. She is discovered. Let her go!
Catherine (*after a beat; falteringly*) Of whom, sir, do you speak?
General The carriage will be waiting for you at the stable door. Eleanor, control yourself; you are a fool. (*To Catherine*) You, pack your bags. If you are in my house a minute after seven, I shall not seem so patient then.

And he pushes Eleanor out of the room ahead of him, and marches her away

A stunned silence

Scene 20

Farewells

Chimes for seven o'clock ring out, very slow, very drear. While they do so:

Catherine (*murmuring; dazed*) Turned away. Like this. No reason. No apology. Abrupt, rude, insulting. I shall not see Henry again. Not even a farewell. So uncivil, so unkind. I must go at seven, so the General does not have to see me. Why? Why?

The clock finishes chiming

A servant brings two little suitcases and puts them down beside Catherine, who picks them up and carries them to the carriage. She sits, staring straight ahead. The sound of rain. Catherine gets wet

Eleanor appears, clutching an umbrella

Eleanor Write to me, Catherine! Let me know that you are safe! Write to me here and — I must ask it — under cover to my maid.
Catherine No, Eleanor, if you are not allowed to receive a letter from me, I am sure I had better not write.

They hug

Eleanor runs off, in tears

Scene 21

Going Home

We hear the noise of the carriage

The Light is still stark and unsympathetic. Narrators comment, and Catherine hears voices from the past.

Mr Morland The road she now travelled was the same which she had so happily passed along to Woodston.
Catherine (*to herself, quietly*) Why?
James She was too wretched to be fearful.
Catherine Why?
James Every mile added to her sufferings.
Catherine Why?
Mrs Allen At Woodston, the General himself had given her the most positive conviction of his actually wishing their marriage.
General I trust that it will very speedily be furnished: it waits only for a lady's taste!
Tilney Another thought came to her. How would Henry think and feel and look when he returned to Northanger and heard of her being gone?
Catherine Why?

James She felt no eagerness for her journey's conclusion. What had she to say that would not simply extend a useless resentment? She could never do justice to Henry's merit.

Mr Morland Her father, mother and baby Harriet were there to welcome her.

Scene 22

Fullerton Again

The Morlands gather round Catherine. We hear a confused chorus of "Welcome home ... How wet you look ... How we have missed you ... Are you quite well?"

The Lights warm a little

Catherine Reluctantly and with much hesitation did she begin an explanation.

There is a shocked silence

Mr Morland But such a long and lonely journey!

Mrs Morland And by yourself! Oh, Catherine, it could have been most unpleasant for you.

Mr Morland Your mother and I would never have allowed this. General Tilney has acted neither as a gentleman nor as a parent.

Mrs Morland I am sorry for his children. They must have a sad time of it. But it is no matter now — Catherine is safe at home. And now it is all over, perhaps there is no great harm done. It is always good for young people to be put upon, exerting themselves: and you know, my dear, you always were a sad little shatter-brained creature ...

Mrs Morland rushes off to separate two squabbling children

Catherine (*calling off; hopelessly*) But why? Oh, Mama, why did he do it? I cannot understand.

Mr Morland (*to us*) For two days we watched her. She could neither sit still, nor employ herself for ten minutes together. In her silence and her sadness she was the very reverse of all that she had been before.

Catherine sinks to the floor

Mrs Morland And then a letter came!

Catherine From Eleanor!

Scene 23

The Forge

Catherine (*reciting the letter*) "What can I tell you? I am shut out from every explanation. But I know that after Henry's return, he and my father conversed in the most unfriendly manner. I did not understand much of what either said —— "

As she reads, Tilney and the General come forward in mid-fracas. Their argument rages around her

General You will obey me, sir, you will *obey* me!
Tilney I know my duty to you sir, my duty is to urge you, beg you to consider the improper, inexcusable intentions that have driven you in this.
General How dare you lecture me. A boy, that's all you are, sir. What do you *know*? My reasons are my own, and for my family's interest.
Tilney Not for *my* interest. I disown your reasons.
General I order you to acquiesce in them!
Tilney You shall not force me to embrace injustice. My conscience ——
General How dare you speak to me of conscience!
Tilney What of your own? Where is your conscience, sir? How could you treat Miss Morland as you have, how could your seeming courtesy be driven by so base a motive? How could your cruelty find so shameful a spur?
General You put yourself in danger, sir. My actions are my own, my motives are not yours or any man's to question. Think carefully before you speak again. You know that I can do much more, much *worse* than send a beggar packing. Your living comes to you from me, and I can take it back again. I warn you, sir!
Tilney I am ashamed to hear you threaten me ——
General Pack up your shame, sir, with your baggage. We leave for Hereford tonight.
Tilney I leave for Woodston. You shall not hinder me.
General If you dare cross me ——
Tilney I do. I will. Good-night, sir.

Scene 24

Tea and Sympathy

The two men part. Catherine crushes the letter

Mrs Allen sweeps in with a chair, which she places near Catherine

Mrs Allen I really have not patience with the General! Do you think these silk gloves wear very well? I put them on new the first time we visited the Upper Rooms. Oh, Bath is a very nice place, Catherine, is it not? But you know, you and I were quite forlorn at first.
Catherine Yes. But that did not last long ——
Mrs Allen Very true. We soon met Mrs Thorpe and then we wanted for nothing. Do you remember that evening?
Catherine I do! Oh, perfectly.
Mrs Allen (*tactless as ever*) It was very agreeable, was it not? Mr Tilney drank tea with us, and I always thought him a great addition.

Catherine gulps and turns away

(*After a moment, wandering away*) I really have not patience with the General. Such an agreeable, worthy man as he seemed to be. I vow ——

Mrs Allen exits

Catherine (*cutting across*) And then another letter came.
Isabella From Isabella Thorpe!

SCENE 25

The Worm Turns

Isabella glides forwards

Isabella (*chilly*) Dear Catherine, I am sorry that you do not wish to write to me. After our many weeks of friendship, after so many confidences and declarations — on my part, at least — of loyalty, I own myself surprised. I had not thought a woman capable of such inconstancy. To show I still reserve a tender thought for you, I know that I must write to tell you of a sadness. Two days ago in London, my brother took me to the Bedford, and there we met old General Tilney. A most unhappy conversation crossed between them, which I fear may injure you …

Again, this scene plays around Catherine, still sitting on the floor. We hear the tipsy comments of Thorpe's drinking companions

John (*drunkenly*) Rich? Old Morland! No, not he!
General But surely, sir, you told me ——
John I was deceived. Thought they were wealthy. I was quite mistaken.

Act II, Scene 26

James, the son, bragged of his parents' wealth. A vain pretender. Boasted of his father's acres, said he was a man of substance! Man of straw, more like.

General (*thunderously*) But did you not enquire? You told me you had seen his property, visited his farms, ridden for half a day round his estate!

John (*nervously*) I told you I had heard of 'em, you told me I had been there.

General The wealthy aunt?

John Dead and in debt.

General And Catherine — his *only* daughter?

John One of ten or twelve!

General And Morland's private fortune?

John It would not keep a lame mare from the shambles.

General You spoke of thousands, sir, of tens of thousands!

John The son told me of more! And Morland, too! For when my sister here was engaged to marry James, his father promised them a fortune — livings in Wiltshire worth thousands! But I asked him, "What's it worth?" and then we had the truth. Less then a pigsty on a salt marsh, less than a hovel in a hedgerow. The family, sir, are indigent, numerous beyond example, by no means respected in their neighbourhood, aiming at a style of life their fortune cannot warrant and seeking to better themselves by wealthy connections. A *forward, bragging, scheming* race.

General I have been deceived! Grossly deceived! Betrayed! Made a fool of! I was led to understand her worth a fortune! I was told she had a settlement of ten or fifteen thousand pounds. Why! I have fed her, housed her, followed her around like an innocent, listening to her prattle of her father's land, his hothouses, his tenants, his gardens! How she has *wearied* me with tales of his property. How I have been deceived!

Scene 26

Despair

Isabella, the General, John, Mrs Morland, Mrs Allen and James gather in the shadows. They speak to Catherine

Isabella (*with great satisfaction*) You have been *greatly* wronged.

General I shall turn her out. Out in the street where she belongs.

Isabella I tried to argue with him, but he was deaf to all reason. So typical of the male sex. I despise them all. Poor Catherine. How sad you must be…

John Vipers and weasels! And she's the worst!

General Imposters, swindlers and frauds! The girl's a fake.

Mrs Morland You always were a sad little shatter-brained creature.

Mrs Allen You never saw a better bred man than the General in your life! What can you have done to make him treat you so?
James Oh, Catherine, beware how you give your heart!
Isabella (*slipping away*) I remain your true but abandoned friend, Isabella Thorpe.
Catherine (*a great cry*) I DID BELIEVE THAT HENRY LOVED ME! I can never forget him, or think of him with less tenderness than I do now. But he might forget me. And if we met…

There is a sound effect of doors slamming shut

Catherine lies in a heap, listless and utterly demoralized

There is a long, uncomfortable silence. Then there is a knock on an offstage door. Catherine ignores the sound. She cannot move. Another knock. A pause, then four or five knocks

   Tilney enters and stands near Catherine. She looks up and sees him

In the background, music begins. Colour creeps back into the lighting

SCENE 27

Joy

Tilney (*formally*) Miss Morland?
Catherine (*faintly*) Mr Tilney.
Tilney I have arrived from Woodston. I must explain. My father ——
Catherine I know. I heard it all.
Tilney Not all. (*A beat*) I must tell you that his anger, though it did shock, could not, would not intimidate me. I was sustained in my purpose by the justice of my cause. I was bound in honour to you, in honour and in love. My father himself had urged me to win your heart, an enterprise for which I had needed no encouragement, and I think, I pray that heart is mine. The withdrawal of my father's consent, of his indulgence, of his blessing, the severest threats of his unreasonable anger, cannot shake my fidelity, my love for you, Miss Morland. (*A beat*) Will you be my wife?

The music swells. Tilney helps Catherine get to her feet

SCENE 28

Finale

The other characters join Catherine and Tilney

Act II, Scene 28

Mr Morland Mr and Mrs Morland's surprise on being applied to by Mr Tilney for their consent to his marrying their daughter was, for a few minutes, considerable!
Mrs Allen But as nothing after all could be more natural than Catherine's being beloved, they confessed themselves without a single objection.
James They *did* require that General Tilney should approve. His consent was all that they wished for.
Catherine Catherine and Henry parted ——
Tilney And waited ——
Catherine — and waited.
Isabella What circumstances could possibly work upon a temper like the General's?

Eleanor arrives in full bridal wear

Eleanor The circumstance which chiefly availed was the marriage of his daughter with a man of fortune and consequence. (*Confidentially*) Her partiality for this gentleman was not of a recent origin, but he had long been withheld by the General from addressing her by the inferiority of his station.
General However, his unexpected accession to title and fortune removed every difficulty!
Eleanor The influence of the Viscount — and Vicomtess (*the others applaud her new position*) in their brother's behalf ——
Mr Morland — was assisted by the news that Catherine would have three thousand pounds.
General This greatly contributed to smooth the descent of the General's pride, and very quickly he gave his consent.
Catherine Henry and Catherine were married, the bells rang, and everybody smiled ——
General — and perhaps the General's interference, far from being injurious to their happiness, improved their knowledge of each other, and added strength to their attachment.
Tilney So we leave it to be settled by whoever it may concern, whether the tendency of this story be altogether to recommend parental tyranny, or reward filial disobedience.

Tilney and Catherine embrace. And the company dance together; the eighth set piece [See Music Plot]

The Lights burn brightly and petals drop

CURTAIN

FURNITURE AND PROPERTY LIST

Only the furniture and properties mentioned in the text are listed here. Further items may be added at the director's discretion

ACT I

On stage: Muslin cloth

Off stage: Books (**Catherine**)
3-candle candelabra (**Isabella**)
Five chairs (**Stage Management**)
Whip and reins for Thorpe (**Stage Management**)
Bags (**James**)

Personal: **Isabella**: pocket book

ACT II

On stage: Bags for **Servants**
Umbrellas for **Servants**
Chest containing pillows
Cabinet containing scrolls

Off stage: Bed (**Stage Management**)
Lamp (**Catherine**)
Books (**Catherine** and **Isabella**)
Candle (**Annette**)
Letter (**Tilney**)
Letter (**Isabella**)
Basket of flowers (**Servant Girl**)
Umbrella (**Eleanor**)
Chair (**Mrs Allen**)
Petals (**Stage Management**)

LIGHTING PLOT

Practical fittings required: none
Property fittings required: candelabra, chandelier
Various interior and exterior settings

ACT I

To open: Covering spot on candelabra

Cue 1	Music *Sudden rush of candlelight over centre of stage;* *flickering flame effect*	(Page 1)
Cue 2	**Isabella** blows out a candle on the candelabra *Dim covering spot slightly; dancing shadow effect*	(Page 2)
Cue 3	**Isabella** blows out the second candle *Dim covering spot more*	(Page 2)
Cue 4	**Isabella** blows out the last candle *Snap off covering spot*	(Page 2)
Cue 5	**Catherine**: " ... his fierce and haughty breast —— " *Bring up light on* **Montoni**	(Page 3)
Cue 6	**Montoni**: "You may know that I am not to be trifled with." *Snap off light on* **Montoni**	(Page 3)
Cue 7	Cloth flutters down on **Catherine** *Cross-fade to Fullerton setting*	(Page 4)
Cue 8	**Venetian/Tilney** approaches *Flicker and dip light*	(Page 9)
Cue 9	**Isabella**: " ... who shall be nameless ..." *Bring down house lights on onstage theatre*	(Page 17)
Cue 10	**Dimity**: " ... his companions, and his horse." *Bring up lights to daytime setting*	(Page 19)
Cue 11	Chandelier descends *Change lights to indoor setting with covering* *lights on chandelier*	(Page 21)

Cue 12	**Mrs Allen**: "Do *just* as you please, my dear." *Cross-fade lights to carriage setting*	(Page 26)
Cue 13	**John**: " ... their damned necks!" *Change lights to indoor setting with cover on chandelier and candlelight effect*	(Page 28)
Cue 14	**John** exits in pursuit of **Catherine** *Cross-fade lights to **Catherine**'s lodgings*	(Page 32)
Cue 15	**Tilney**: " ... Beechen Cliff." *Bring up deep golden sunshine effect*	(Page 35)
Cue 16	Tilneys go *Fade out sunshine effect; general lighting*	(Page 37)
Cue 17	**Isabella** dances round; the Tilneys drift by *Bring up lights to indoor setting with chandelier cover*	(Page 41)
Cue 18	**Tilney** and **Catherine** join the dance *Bring lights up brighter, then slowly fade, leaving single spot on James; then fade to black-out*	(Page 48)

ACT II

To open:	General dim exterior lighting with rain effect	
Cue 19	**Tilney**: "No, certainly." Beat *Dim lights slightly*	(Page 50)
Cue 20	**James**: " ... the one virtue you admire is constancy!" *Cross-fade to **Catherine**'s bedroom with firelight and moving shadow effects; covering spot on lamp*	(Page 53)
Cue 21	**Catherine**: "What could possibly disturb a person's calm?" *Shift lights to reveal large cabinet*	(Page 54)
Cue 22	**Catherine**: "Oh no oh no oh no!" *Flicker covering light on lamp, then cut light as lamp goes out*	(Page 55)
Cue 23	Banging and moaning, howling, rattling *Bring up lights brightly*	(Page 55)
Cue 24	**The General** and **Eleanor** arrive *Brighten lights to suggest March exterior*	(Page 57)

Lighting Plot

Cue 25	**The General** leaves *Change lights to suggest dark, woody, green place*	(Page 58)
Cue 26	**Catherine**: "Emily?" *Change lights; interior lighting*	(Page 59)
Cue 27	**General**: "Persuasive, don't you think?" *Change lights to indicate moving into room* US	(Page 59)
Cue 28	**General**: "The Library!" *Change lights to indicate moving into room* L	(Page 59)
Cue 29	**General**: "The Cloister!" *Change lights again*	(Page 60)
Cue 30	**General**: "Let us pass on ——" *Change lights again*	(Page 60)
Cue 31	**Catherine** sits and is joined by **Eleanor** *Spooky back-lighting*	(Page 61)
Cue 32	**Catherine**: "Good-night." *Black-out*	(Page 62)
Cue 33	**Annette** comes forward with a candle *Bring up covering spot on candle*	(Page 62)
Cue 34	Loud cock-crow *Bring up bright, sunny lighting*	(Page 63)
Cue 35	**Catherine** and **Annette** set off *Fade sunny lighting; bring up dim lighting on Mrs Tilney's room*	(Page 64)
Cue 36	**Catherine** throws back imaginary curtains *Bring up bright lighting from direction of curtains*	(Page 64)
Cue 37	**Catherine** runs to her room *Cross-fade lights to* **Catherine**'s *room setting*	(Page 65)
Cue 38	**Catherine**: "No!" *Sudden change of light*	(Page 66)
Cue 39	**General**: " See for yourself, Miss Morland." Music *Dappled light*	(Page 70)

Cue 40	During **Catherine**'s speech beginning "Never has a day passed so quickly!" *Slowly cross-fade lights to **Catherine**'s bedroom setting, with fireglow and candlelight effects*	(Page 71)
Cue 41	**Catherine** carries her bags to the carriage *Stark, unsympathetic lighting with rain effect*	(Page 73)
Cue 42	The Morlands gather round **Catherine** *Increase warmth of lighting*	(Page 74)
Cue 43	**Isabella**, **the General** et al gather round **Catherine** *Switch to colourless, shadowy lighting*	(Page 77)
Cue 44	Music begins *Make lighting more colourful*	(Page 78)
Cue 45	Company dance together *Bring up lighting very bright*	(Page 79)

EFFECTS PLOT

ACT I

Cue 1	As play begins *Music*	(Page 1)
Cue 2	**Isabella**: " ... here they are in my pocket book." *Gothic sound effects (see text p. 1)*	(Page 1)
Cue 3	**Isabella** blows out the first candle *Twinkle of spooky notes*	(Page 2)
Cue 4	**Annette**: "Signora Laurentina ——— " *Far-off cry: "Signora Laurentina."*	(Page 3)
Cue 5	**Annette**: "Signor Montoni." *His name is echoed*	(Page 3)
Cue 6	**Annette** vanishes *Echo effect on **Annette**'s voice, fading*	(Page 3)
Cue 7	Light goes out on **Montoni** *Door bangs; distant echoes; groans; cries of* *"Signora Laurentina" with music underscoring*	(Page 4)
Cue 8	Lights snap to Fullerton *Birds twitter, children squeal and giggle, dog barks*	(Page 4)
Cue 9	**Catherine**: "Bath!" *Music*	(Page 6)
Cue 10	**Catherine**: "Within two days, they arrived!" *Distant music and bustle*	(Page 6)
Cue 11	**Dimity**: " ... and again upon the Friday!" *Burst of music and noise of Upper Rooms*	(Page 7)
Cue 12	**Mrs Allen** and **Catherine** sit *Lessen volume of music*	(Page 8)

Cue 13	Lights flicker and dip *Mysterious tremor of music*	(Page 9)
Cue 14	**Catherine**: " ...a gentle murmur of applause." *Applause*	(Page 9)
Cue 15	**Tilney**: "It may take us nearer to the door" *Music*	(Page 10)
Cue 16	**Catherine** and **Tilney** sit *Lessen volume of music*	(Page 10)
Cue 17	**Isabella**: "Dear, dear Miss Morland!" *Music*	(Page 15)
Cue 18	**Catherine**: "Of course!" *Music*	(Page 16)
Cue 19	**Isabella** and **Catherine** arrive at the theatre *Musical instruments tuning up*	(Page 17)
Cue 20	The fight rages round **Catherine** and **Isabella** *Sudden blast of post horn*	(Page 18)
Cue 21	Lights switch *Street noise. Horses whinnying*	(Page 19)
Cue 22	Chandelier descends *Music*	(Page 21)
Cue 23	**James**: " — I know she will not mind it." *Music*	(Page 22)
Cue 24	**Isabella**: "What a delightful girl!" *Music*	(Page 24)
Cue 25	**Mrs Allen**: "Do *just* as you please, my dear." *Music*	(Page 26)
Cue 26	**John**: "LET HIM GO!" *Very gentle trotting noises*	(Page 26)
Cue 27	**John**: " ... a little behind his left ear ..." *Horse's hooves speed up for a moment, then subside*	(Page 26)
Cue 28	**Catherine**: " ... could not entirely repress a doubt ——" *Horse's hooves get faster, increasing in speed during following dialogue*	(Page 27)

Effects Plot

Cue 29	**John**: "Three of them broke their damned necks!" *Cut horses hooves; music*	(Page 28)
Cue 30	The dance ends *Cut music*	(Page 28)
Cue 31	Dancers take up positions *Music*	(Page 30)
Cue 32	**Tilney**: " ... a security worth having ..." *Cut music*	(Page 31)
Cue 33	Lights shift to **Catherine**'s lodgings *Hooves and carriages; jolly "off for the day" music*	(Page 32)
Cue 34	**Catherine**: "You have done WHAT?" *Music*	(Page 34)
Cue 35	**Catherine** runs and runs *Abbey bell rings twelve*	(Page 34)
Cue 36	**Tilney**: "The party set out for Beechen Cliff." *Music; an expansive, "noble" theme*	(Page 35)
Cue 37	**Isabella**: " ... quite out of the question." *Sudden chord*	(Page 41)
Cue 38	**Isabella** wanders off *Music in background*	(Page 42)
Cue 39	**Tilney** moves away *Cut music*	(Page 42)
Cue 40	**General**: " ... not wholly disagreeable." *Music*	(Page 44)
Cue 41	**Count de Vereza** appears *Courtly Venetian theme*	(Page 44)
Cue 42	**Count de Vereza** appears *Courtly Venetian theme*	(Page 45)
Cue 43	**Isabella**: " ... where am I wandering to?" *Surge of music, leading to underscore for rest of scene*	(Page 46)
Cue 44	**Catherine**: "To James!" *Cut music*	(Page 47)

Cue 45	**Catherine**: "So difficult." *Music*	(Page 47)

ACT II

Cue 46	As Act II begins *Sound of rain; horses stamp and snort*	(Page 49)
Cue 47	**General**: " ... a full stop loose!" *Trotting hooves*	(Page 49)
Cue 48	Lights dim slightly *Wind gets up*	(Page 50)
Cue 49	**General**: " ... not wholly disagreeable." *Music*	(Page 44)
Cue 50	**Voice** speaks *Voice with echo effect as per text p. 51*	(Page 51)
Cue 51	**Servants** help **Catherine** *and* **Tilney** from the carriage *Music plays, elegant and civilized*	(Page 51)
Cue 52	**General**: "Dinner to be on table directly!" *Cut music*	(Page 52)
Cue 53	Lights switch to **Catherin**e's bedroom setting *Rain and wind against shutters*	(Page 53)
Cue 54	**Catherine**: " ... the wind and rain with awe ..." *Door bangs*	(Page 53)
Cue 55	**Catherine**: " ... I could have answered for my courage ... " *Creepy music*	(Page 53)
Cue 56	**Tilney's Voice** speaks *Dialogue as p. 53-55, including cues 56-58*	(Page 53)
Cue 57	**Catherine** looks round nervously *Clock ticks; eerie music*	(Page 54)
Cue 58	Knock at the door *Music stops abruptly*	(Page 54)
Cue 59	Door shuts on **Catherine** *Creepy music*	(Page 54)

Effects Plot

Cue 60	The Light flickers and goes out *Storm rises; banging and moaning, wind howling, doors rattling*	(Page 55)
Cue 61	**Eleanor**: " ... to my attention." *Gong*	(Page 56)
Cue 62	**Annette** appears in the shadows *Creepy music*	(Page 56)
Cue 63	**Catherine**: " ... take his walk so early ... " *Burst of merry music*	(Page 57)
Cue 64	**Eleanor** runs off, hiding tears *Music*	(Page 59)
Cue 65	Lights switch *Ticking clock*	(Page 60)
Cue 66	Lights switch *Echoey acoustic; iron gate swings open*	(Page 60)
Cue 67	**General**: " Let us pass on ... " *Cut echoey acoustic*	(Page 60)
Cue 68	**Catherine**: " ... mix them at his leisure." *Gong*	(Page 61)
Cue 69	**Annette**: "He will go later." *Bell tolls midnight*	(Page 63)
Cue 70	**Annette** tuts. A few beats *Loud cock-crow*	(Page 63)
Cue 71	**Annette**: "I shall go with you!" *"Edge of seat" music*	(Page 63)
Cue 72	**Annette** and Gothic characters burst in *Creepy music*	(Page 65)
Cue 73	The Gothics look around them *Cut music*	(Page 66)
Cue 74	**Catherine** throws *Udolpho* away *Formal, stately music*	(Page 67)
Cue 75	**Tilney**: "Thank you indeed." *Music begins*	(Page 89)

Cue 76	**General**: "See for yourself, Miss Morland." *Music*	(Page 70)
Cue 77	**Catherine**: " ... but not our comfort ... " *Crash of door slamming shut; cut music*	(Page 71)
Cue 78	The **General** marches **Eleanor** away; a silence *Seven o'clock chimes*	(Page 72)
Cue 79	**Catherine** sits on the carriage *The sound of rain*	(Page 73)
Cue 80	**Eleanor** runs off in tears *Noise of carriage*	(Page 73)
Cue 81	**Catherine**: " And if we met ..." *Doors slamming shut*	(Page 78)
Cue 82	**Catherine** looks up and sees **Tilney** *Music*	(Page 78)
Cue 83	**Tilney**: "Will you be my wife?" *Music swells*	(Page 78)
Cue 84	**Tilney** and **Catherine** embrace *Music for the dance*	(Page 79)